T0134347

Kai Bronner | Rainer Hirt | Cornelius Ringe (Eds.)

(((ABA)))

AUDIO BRANDING ACADEMY

Yearbook
2012/2013

Nomos

Supported by:

the art and science of effective business sound

www.thesoundagency.com

PRO SOUND EFFECTS
Next Level Libraries, Licensing & Service

manmademusic.com

SONIC BRANDING, MUSIC SUPERVISION, SOUNDTRACK PRODUCTION, PARTNERSHIPS, ORIGINAL COMPOSITION.

Die Deutsche Nationalbibliothek lists this publication in the
Deutsche Nationalbibliografie; detailed bibliographic data
is available in the Internet at http://dnb.d-nb.de.

ISBN 978-3-8329-7878-5

Bildnachweis: © Andres Rodriguez - Fotolia.com

1. Auflage 2013
© Nomos Verlagsgesellschaft Baden-Baden 2013. Printed in Germany.
Alle Rechte, auch die des Nachdrucks von Auszügen, der fotomechanischen
Wiedergabe und der Übersetzung, vorbehalten. Gedruckt auf alterungs-
beständigem Papier.

Prelude

When you read this, you probably aren't holding a book about audio branding for the first time. Over the past few years numerous publications on sound and music in brand communications came out. However, much more important for this unique industry is the growing number of sophisticated audio branding cases with very strategic approaches and holistic interpretation of brand and multisensory design. You can find some of the most inspiring cases in the yearbooks and on the congress-websites of the Audio Branding Academy.

All brands have acoustic emissions. The question is: do they make just any noise or do they have their own appropriate sound? And how long will we have to evangelize the marketing world, education and public in order to establish a natural consciousness for listening?

It is time to present more solutions and real results in the market instead of imposing theoretical capabilities. Too often we see great audio branding strategies with a comprehensive brand sound concept and well designed guidelines, but with no consequent implementation. So something that too many cases still have to prove is relevance. Only when people can hear the difference in everyday life will audio branding get the status it deserves: a complimentary standard tool of brand management.

By establishing the Audio Branding Award, we want to support the industry to meet this challenge by promoting transparent competition of best practice. To be eligible for the award one must disclose the audio branding strategy and architecture of the brand sound concept. But to win it the results must convince the audience without explanations. Why? Because this is reality!

One of the central aims of the Audio Branding Academy is to foster exchange between scientists, scholars, students, practitioners and ex-

perts in the field of audio branding and to establish a general consciousness for sound and music in brand communications. This mission has
been confirmed by the results of the Audio Branding Barometer 2011, as
it showed a strong desire for more exchange between scientist and practitioners. Already 83.3 % of audio branding suppliers regularly read scientific texts for continuous improvement of their services. No wonder
that there is an overwhelming consensus on the benefits of scientific approaches for audio branding. But also science and education discover
more and more the field of audio branding and value the insights they
gain from the growing exchange with practitioners.

In order to take these circumstances into account, the Audio Branding
Academy developed a concept for its hybrid congresses as the combina-
tion of academic symposiums and business conventions with best prac-
tice cases and its own award. Therefore we were more than happy when
Professor Charles Spence invited us to cooperate with the University of
Oxford and to run the Audio Branding Congress 2012 in the prestigious
Oxford Examination Schools. Against the background of our host and
witnessing the fact that audio branding suppliers are highly interested in
scientific matters and approaches, the event was focused with the motto
"Listen To Consumers."

In this Yearbook you will find the proceedings of the Audio Branding
Congress 2012 with a comprehensive summary article, impressive jury-
selected award case studies of brands like Nokia, Dell, Harrods, and The
Linde Group, an article of keynote speaker Professor Charles Spence
about the future of synaesthetic marketing, contributions from the scientific Call for Papers 2012, and a documentation of the market survey Audio Branding Barometer 2012 among others.

We want to express our deepest gratitude to all the speakers, the scientific advisory board, many helping hands, our supporters and partners
who have made this Congress possible. The Audio Branding Academy
had the pleasure to trust in the decision of an internationally experienced award jury: Carl-Frank Westermann, Alex Moulton, Patrick
Langeslag, Daniel M. Jackson, Professor Florian Käppler and Martyn
Ware.

Special thanks go to Professor Charles Spence and Dr. Klemens Knöferle for hosting the Congress at the University of Oxford and to Julian Treasure for being an eloquent moderator. Last but not least we thank our sponsors Pro Sound Effects, Man Made Music and The Sound Agency.

Cornelius Ringe, Kai Bronner, Rainer Hirt
Hamburg, March 2013

Contents

Call for Papers 2012

Audio Branding Congress 2012 Summary

Alex Moulton

eyeball

Introduction

The fourth annual Audio Branding Congress was held on December 11, 2012 at Oxford University. Attendees gathered on a crisp wintery day at the beautiful Oxford Examination Schools building in anticipation of an engaging day of presentations, discussions and socializing. With dozens of return attendees and a large number of new faces, this year boasted the largest attendance and greatest international representation in the four years of the Audio Branding Congress.

Witnessing demand within the audio branding industry for increased emphasis on market research, testing and validation, the Audio Branding Academy focused the event with the motto "Listen To Consumers." Audio Branding Academy founders Dr. Cornelius Ringe, Kai Bronner and Rainer Hirt welcomed the audience and thanked the supporters, partners and Oxford University hosts. With only a hint of irony, Ringe explained that they had listened to their own consumers in choosing the event theme after receiving excellent feedback from past years.

The Academy's mission to foster exchange between scientists, scholars, students, practitioners and experts has grown substantially year upon year. After the 2011 Congress held at Columbia University, New York City, where 15 countries were represented, Ringe announced that this Congress included attendees from a record 21 countries.

Next to be introduced was Julian Treasure, moderator for the day's proceedings. An eminent sound expert, author and chairman of The Sound Agency, Treasure welcomed the audience warmly and delivered an engaging introductory talk on the importance of listening. Even with noise pollution becoming an increasingly significant issue, Treasure noted that brands are often tempted to "shout over their competition" in attempts to stand out. Referencing several related studies and empirical evidence about cluttered sound environments, Treasure challenged the room of audio branding industry experts to be "champions of listening."

Julian Treasure

Enhancing Multisensory Experiences and Brands Through Sound

Co-host and returning speaker Professor Charles Spence took the stage, ready to update the eager audience with his latest research. Representing the Oxford University Department of Experimental Psychology, Professor Spence has established his Crossmodal Research Lab as a leading source of research on the confluence of cognitive neuroscience and marketing.

Diving quickly into a survey of practical, real-world examples of using sound to enhance product experience, Professor Spence began with recent developments within the food industry. Citing examples such as New York chef Zakary Pelaccio's playful pairings of recipes with songs, or Spence's own "Sound of the Sea" experiments at The Fat Duck restaurant in conjunction with audio branding company Condiment Junkie. Spence also shared a collection of sonic and crossmodal cues found in current print advertising campaigns.

Charles Spence

The Crossmodal Research Lab has produced fascinating research linking specific tastes in the human palate to notes, chords and musical arrangements. Professor Spence has also found commonalities across species, noting similar hedonic and aversive reactions in human babies, chimpanzees and even mice.

With growing demand in the marketplace for enhanced gastronomic experiences, Professor Spence reported more intriguing trends; expert bartender "mixologists" pairing music with drinks, a "gin & sonic" created by a chef specializing in molecular gastronomy, a mobile app produced in conjunction with his department that enhances the flavour of potato crisps and even a chef who is experimenting with serving dishes on a mobile tablet device to create a synesthetic dining experience. Spence predicts more multisensory products and experiential advertising for the near future as marketers and producers seek to create new and exciting experiences for their consumers.

The Role of Consumer Research in Audio Branding

The second presentation of the day was given by Professor Nancy Puccinelli of Oxford University's Saïd Business School. Turning the conversation from the experimental use of sound to the more pragmatic approach of the advertising industry, Professor Puccinelli presented a wide body of research in the field of social psychology.

Nancy Puccinelli

Citing her studies on the persuasive power of music along with consulting work for major international brands, Professor Puccinelli impressed upon the audience that carefully considered music choices based on mood, instrumentation and arrangement can successfully enhance audience perception of a product. Equally important was her finding that incongruous music used in TV advertising has a range of effects on the audience, from no effect at all to a detrimental, disengaging emotional response.

Professor Puccinelli next summarized her continuing research on the congruity of sound in marketing. With recent studies based around the use of music to induce consumer mood and choice, along with current research on the critical importance of sound during retail promotional periods, she gave insightful examples of how brands should pay particular attention to sound in point of purchase environments. Recounting specifics on the use of holiday-themed music in shopping areas, her research has lead her to believe that holiday music can overwhelm consumers and hurt sales. Her hope is that this important finding should encourage brands to pay more attention to the mood and psychological perceptions of their purchase environments.

Audio Branding Barometer 2012

Returning to the Congress as a representative of the Audio Branding Academy, Dr. Klaus Frieler shared the results of the 2012 Audio Branding Barometer. Conducted online in September/October 2012, the study gathered market data from 33 agencies in 12 countries, a similar sample size to previous years.

The results showed continued growth from a nascent industry. Most agencies offering audio branding services are still under 10 years old, half starting within the past six years, while employing under 20 people. 95% of budgets remain under USD $100,000 but revenues were up by a third and agencies are optimistic about continued growth.

Along with other compelling data collected on evolving business models and service offerings, the basic definition of the term "audio branding" is also in flux. Participants in the survey placed more emphasis this year on process, strategy and identity without relying on comparisons to the world of visual branding. Dr. Frieler's interpretation of this new direction was that as the practice of audio branding continues to grow in perceived significance around the world, audio branding companies are becoming more confident about their field and the relevance of their offerings to clients.

Klaus Frieler

Product-Related Sounds Speed up Visual Search

Dr. Klemens Knöferle, co-host and colleague of Professor Charles Spence, presented the Oxford University Crossmodal Research Lab's current findings on consumers' experiences in visually cluttered environments. Recent studies show that shoppers are only able to process a very small fraction of the visual stimuli presented to them. This fact, combined with increasing numbers of product choices, sums up the types of new challenges that marketers are faced with to make their products stand out. Knöferle's team was curious to discover how the effects of sensory modalities other than vision – primarily audio cues – could facilitate in the visual search for objects in a retail setting.

By creating a number of tests to measure the effects of sound and scent, Knöferle has collected data that supports his theory that logical and intentional multisensory cues can decrease visual search time. Revealing the power of intentional sound, Knöferle shared a 2010 study that found decreased reaction times when a logical sound was paired with a visual stimulus, while response time with no sound at all is relatively close to that of a distracting or illogical sound pairing.

Klemens Knöferle

Knöferle's tests are designed around playing congruent, incongruent, unrelated sounds, or no sound at all and measuring visual search times and accuracy. As the previously cited study found, he was able to decrease participants' reaction times significantly by pairing congruent sounds with images of standard supermarket items. He also reinforced the finding that unrelated or incongruent sounds resulted in equal performance as no sound, showing that sound has little distracting effect.

Giving a glimpse of the future, Knöferle promised that the Crossmodal Research Lab's future studies will continue to question these findings, potentially looking at the effects of audio logos in retail environments, verbal and semantic auditory cues and applications of new eye tracking technology.

Implicit and Explicit Effects of Music on Brand Perception in TV Ads

Wrapping up the morning's presentations was Dr. Daniel Müllensiefen of Goldsmiths, University Of London, sharing his team's research produced in tandem with London advertising agency adam&eveDDB. Müllensiefen opened with a powerful summary of research describing the power of music in advertising to convey brand image, increase recall, heighten effectiveness and create emotional bonds between brands and consumers. Previous work in the fields of social and occupational psychology, along with more recent neuropsychology advances, have led his group to explore the subject matter from a different angle using cognitive and perceptual psychology, specifically examining music priming.

Daniel Müllensiefen

After poking fun at the typical advertising agency music creative brief, replete with contradictions and phrases that have lost meaning with repetition, Müllensiefen described his process for arriving at a more scientific and quantitative method of selecting or creating music that would have the intended emotional effect. The first experiment polled 185 participants, mapping mood characteristics of 16 potential music selections. The data was used to chart the semantic differential and measure the closeness between each song and the brand goals. The second experiment evaluated the effects of congruent and incongruent music with qualitative focus testing and recall testing.

The results of both experiments create a convincing body of evidence to show the measurable results of intentional music choices, not the least of which was that "congruent music makes an ad 16% more effective." Müllensiefen enthusiastically pointed to this statistic alone being powerful enough to shift brands' perception of the importance of sound in a marketplace where every effectiveness gain translates to larger ROI.

Award Case Study: Nokia

Henry Daw, Principal Sound Designer at Nokia presented the first award case study of the afternoon. After the massive success of Nokia's crowd-sourced ringtone initiative – presented at the 2011 Congress by Nokia colleague Tapio Hakanen – Daw explained the challenges faced by his team to further increase international product and brand relevance. The key, as Daw explained, was to focus on local markets and encourage more consumer engagement.

Nokia has continued to emphasize the importance of large quantitative user studies, allowing Daw's group to gather data about ringtone popularity, preferences and usage habits to validate ringtone selections. Through analysing this feedback, Nokia was able to balance focus between global content and region-specific content. This also precipitated the need for a survey of many local music cultures and listening habits in different regions of the world.

As the result of this research, Nokia launched a new crowd-sourced initiative called "Regional Ringtones, Designed By You" with a substantial cash grand prize and five smaller prizes for each of the 5 focus regions: China, India, Middle East & Africa, South East Asia & Pacific and Latin America. The program was deemed a success, with 1,500 total entries from 474 local musicians and sound designers.

Award Case Study: Globosat

Representing Rio de Janeiro-based music branding company GOMUS, Natalia Lannes and Guilherme Flarys described the enormous challenge presented by their client Globosat. To revolutionize the process of music discovery and licensing for the largest pay TV broadcast group in Latin America, GOMUS had to create a new audio style guide for each channel along with a universally accessible and easy-to-use music database.

After an overview of the enormous range of music already available to network producers, Flarys explained the nuances and unique challenges of creating a unified searchable music catalogue. GOMUS also gathered and pre-cleared new music from major publishers, creating relationships for Globosat that would allow easier synch licensing of newly released music. Flarys also gave an overview of their new music management interface and intuitive search tools for non-musicians.

Lannes took the audience through several examples of how the new brand guide would create unity and consistency across the Globosat brands while clearly defining the sound of each channel. GOMUS identified the musical DNA of each sub-brand and created straightforward language for network producers to meet these criteria. This process also involved curating playlists to help guide music searches and train employees for making intentional choices. The result was a more objective approach to music selection, clearly defined identity guidelines and an entirely new, efficient synch licensing process.

Award Case Study: DKSH

On behalf of Berlin-based agency kleiner und bold Alexander Wodrich, founder of Wodrich Audio Branding in Berlin, was hired to rebrand DKSH, a leading Swiss company that helps their clients expand business and distribution across Asian markets. His initial challenge was to gain insight on the musical listening habits and cultural touchpoints within each market that DKSH services in order to more clearly define a sonic palette that would resonate with the client's wide audience. Wodrich's research presented a survey of traditional musical instrumentation for each region of Asia, along with genre-specific breakdowns for popular music styles. He concluded that while traditional Asian music is highly important and coexists with contemporary styles, most Asian cultures have embraced popular Western music genres and production techniques. Although languages may change, he found that Western-sounding pop music is now a unifying musical connector among Asian subcultures.

After identifying the tonality and emotional differentiators unique to DKSH, Wodrich's goal was to blend the brand's Swiss heritage with its Asian affinity. He settled on a palette of sounds and instruments that could balance both sides of the equation and resonate as both Western and Asian. In addition to composing musical elements that included an audio logo and thematic mood score, Wodrich also cast new talent as the voice of DKSH in order to complete the audio brand.

Award Case Study: Renfe

To define the audio brand for Renfe, a major Spanish train operator with a recently launched new visual identity, Juan Corrales of Madrid-based Flyabit was faced with several intriguing challenges. In order to give shape to a mother brand whose image had been "cannibalized" by its more well-known sub-brands, as well as deploying new branded sound assets across an array of touchpoints, Corrales first defined a new sonic DNA based on the values and goals of the parent organization.

Corrales arrived at the finding that a central theme first needed to be established from which all other brand elements could be derived, most notably the sound logo. Based on a musical motif from the brand anthem, the sound logo could "speak with different voices" by changing the musical arrangements and instrumentation. Beyond melodic instruments, Corrales was inspired by his background as a percussionist to inject a rhythmic element that would also resonate with the transportation brand. The new assets were implemented across a range of media such as advertising, web, corporate communications, point of sale and call centers, as well as the trains themselves. Faced with making audio sound excellent and carry the intended emotional resonance while coming from small, low-fidelity PA speakers of the trains proved to be particularly difficult. The solution Corrales settled on was to reduce the audio information to its simplest form and carefully select the musical arrangement to keep in mind the transmitted frequencies and acoustic properties of train cabins.

Award Case Study: Harrods

The Brand Sense Agency and The Sound Agency, both based in London, U.K., were hired in tandem to strategize and implement a new approach to environmental sound at London's famed department store Harrods. Presenting on behalf of the agencies were Lydia Watson and Tim Hirst. With one million square feet of retail space, an enormous demographic of international clients and a historic brand legacy, the group set a goal to be the most innovative retail-focused sound branding initiative in the world.

After an audit of the entire Harrods store, where sound levels, existing music practices, technical capabilities and shopping habits were meticulously recorded, the branding team understood their challenge to be even greater than previously anticipated. They created a plan to completely overhaul the store's sound capabilities, from installing new speakers capable of focused sound projection to software controls allowing generative and potentially interactive sound fields, along with new aesthetic guidelines for the creation of the sound itself.

Beginning with the toy department, which encompasses several uniquely themed spaces, a test run of strategic implementation was undertaken. By clearly defining each spatial experience, which ranged from an enchanted forest to an alien spacecraft, and overseeing installation, testing and support, a unique experience was created for consumers that reinforced the brand image. After the success of the initial launch, The Brand Sense Agency and The Sound Agency are currently planning and implementing a continued rollout of experiential sound design for additional Harrods departments.

Award Case Study: Dell

Susan Aminoff represented Elias Arts to introduce the agency's multi-year engagement with Dell to create a new global audio identity system. In order to refocus the brand from a product-based computer company to a service-based technology company, Aminoff and her team began with in-depth research to create the foundation from which to rebuild the brand. While many fascinating outcomes of this research and the resulting executions were shared with the attending audience, Dell has requested that details be limited to the presentation itself since the initiative has yet to be launched to the public.

Suffice to say, Elias Arts was able to take their client through an impressive level of engagement on all levels of the organization in order to discover, audit, plan, implement, educate and train Dell employees. Aminoff described the great extent to which she and her team were able to leverage their research and create hundreds of assets, from a central brand thematic and sound logo to an extensive original music library to functional device sounds and more. All elements were audience tested in three global markets, an undertaking that was a very important validation phase for Dell, a company that is well-known for placing significant value on research and consumer feedback.

Most exciting for the attendees, and for the industry itself, was Aminoff's announcement that a training course in audio branding is now a required part of the certification program for all Dell employees and representatives.

Award Case Study: The Linde Group

Richella Odebrecht, Head of Internal Communications and Corporate Branding at Munich-based industrial gas company The Linde Group, was joined by amp co-founders Michele Arnese and Rudi Mauser to present the final case study of the day. Odebrecht explained that for a company that is reshaping itself after numerous successful acquisitions, music was a key driver for building an emotional relationship with the brand across many new employees and diverse local markets. Music was greatly valued by the company's founder Dr. Carl Von Linde and has been an important part of the company's 130 year brand heritage so it was fitting that it form the basis of the company's new internal communications strategy.

Mauser introduced the Linde Theme at its most elementary, a simple four-tone motif composed of notes in the pentatonic scale. Explaining that their goal was to create a short, singable and flexible melody that could work across music styles and transcend cultural boundaries, his experience has led him to believe that singable melodies are the most memorable.

Mauser and Arnese next took the audience on a journey through the arrangements of the theme, from the Linde Masterpiece to the Linde Suite to the resulting brand audio signature. Drawing many parallels between Linde brand values and the finer points of arranging for symphonic orchestra, Mauser described how they were able to express the rich history of the brand. The Linde Suite, an undeniably impressive and inspiring epic, was composed in four movements, each a different style: Romantic, Impressionist, 1960s-inspired and World to take its audience on an auditory journey through history across five continents.

According to Odebrecht, the new Linde audio brand elements have successfully brought employees together and engaged management, resulting in a continued exploration and evolution of brand assets. While the initial project focus was on the Linde Masterpiece, the initiative has continued three years and resulted in the development of an audio logo and signature for the brand

Panel Discussion: Audio Branding: Art, Science or the Art of Science?

The penultimate event of the day was the panel discussion led by moderator Julian Treasure. He was joined by a diverse group of experts: Professor Charles Spence (Oxford University), Alexander Wodrich (Wodrich Audio Branding), Rayan Parikh (Elias Arts), Henry Daw (Nokia), and audio branding consultant Adrion Porter (FusionFlow Media).

Treasure directed the conversation across a range of topics, questioning the panellists about the measurability of sound and how they interpret the results. Spence noted that while the old model of marketing would simply survey opinions and the new model of neuroscience postulates that one should never trust what people say, only what their brain scans communicate, his opinion is that the proper methodology probably lies somewhere in between.

Panel Discussion

Wodrich described how difficult it is to distinguish reactions to audio when so many other sensory factors can come into play. He duly noted that even the mere volume of sound playback can greatly affect the perception and reaction from a test participant or client. Parikh described a recent method that he had used to advance the conversation about sound during a focus group; by asking participants to talk about their favourite music, followed by a discussion on how specific device sounds affect their everyday lives, he was able to open a more nuanced conversation about reactions to sound to get better feedback from his participants.

As the conversation turned to measuring ROI for clients, Porter described the way that he establishes the importance of audio branding for his clients by correlating different factors within an overall brand strategy. Parikh noted that many audio branding initiatives can provide ROI simply by offsetting other marketing costs, not the least of which is expensive music licensing. Wodrich agreed, noting that true measurement of the value of an audio brand can take years and is largely a factor of media budget over time to establish brand recognition.

Arriving at the panel's central theme, Treasure asked his panellists, and then the audience, if they consider themselves artists or scientists or a mix of both. All seemed to be in agreement that a balanced mix of the two approaches is important to arriving at a well-executed audio brand.

Award Ceremony

Award submissions for 2012 came from nine countries on four continents. In advance of the Congress, the expert international judging panel of Daniel M. Jackson, Prof. Florian Käppler, Patrick Langeslag, Alex Moulton, Martyn Ware and Carl-Frank Westermann were involved in two rounds of deadlocked judging, eventually requiring the addition of an extra presentation slot, bringing the total to seven honorees.

Award Ceremony

The new award – a polished metal globe with an auditory "tinkle" when shaken – was unveiled by the ABA founders, along with the news that there would now be 3 awards for Gold, Silver and Bronze. Based on feedback from the first Audio Branding Award presented in 2011, the voting process for 2012 was revised to allow each Congress attendee to cast four individual votes across their favourite case studies.

When the results were announced, the Bronze award went to amp and The Linde Group and the Silver to Wodrich Audio Branding and DKSH. The Gold Award went to The Sound Agency and Brand Sense Agency for Harrods, much to the surprise and delight of moderator Julian Treasure, who led the project for The Sound Agency.

In Conclusion

2012 was a landmark year for our industry. All Congress participants with whom I spoke agreed that the practice of audio branding is only just beginning to take shape. The case studies presented this year were not only inspiring and engaging, but showed a commitment to innovation and the positive transformation of the world we live in.

Hosts and Audio Branding Academy Team

It has been my great honour to participate in growth of the Audio Branding Congress; speaking in Hamburg in 2010, hosting the event in NYC in 2011, judging this year's Award submissions and writing this summary for the past two years have given me a deep appreciation for the passion and dedication of the Audio Branding Academy founders and staff. Moreover, the warm spirit of camaraderie among organizers, the generosity of the speakers and the overwhelming enthusiasm of the attendees who readily share their experience and knowledge are truly unique to this event. While reading the essays and case studies presented in this volume, I would urge you to actively engage in this community via the Audio Branding Academy's website. Reach out to the authors directly to continue the conversation and please consider attending the next Audio Branding Congress. I hope to meet you there.

Alex Moulton
March 2013

Listening to Shoppers

Julian Treasure

The Sound Agency

1. Listening and Brands

Communication has three elements: sending, receiving and a context. Traditionally, marketing has focused on sending, with brands effectively attempting to out-shout one another to get our attention. This has contributed to a very noisy world; one where we are assailed by thousands of branded messages every day, and by a constant cacophony of undesigned, largely unpleasant sound as the wheels of commerce grind loudly around us. As a result, most people have become largely unconscious of the sound around them – and yet it still has major effects on us all, not least in our shopping behaviour. Without careful design, most shopping environments are counter-productive: mindless music and electromechanical noise combine with poor acoustics to produce unpleasant soundscapes that are reducing dwell time, sales and customer satisfaction. The audio branding industry can and should be the world's champion of mindful sound design and conscious listening, thereby making a huge contribution to both economic success and individual wellbeing.

1.1 The Nature of Listening

Listening is a skill, and one that's in danger of dying. Let's define listening as "making meaning from sound". This is the mental process that happens after the physical miracle of hearing. It typically involves pattern recognition (reacting more strongly to frequent or strongly associated sounds), differencing (discounting constant, unchanging sound and focusing on that which moves) and filters. Each individual's listening filters are as unique as that person's fingerprints, retina, face and voice, because the filters are fashioned by all the events and experiences that make up a life.

Figure 1. The main listening filters

Our listening filters start to form before birth (newborn babies have been shown to respond more favourably to their own language patterns than other languages, because we start to hear well before we actually enter the world) and range from the large and social to the specific and very personal or situational. Most people are unaware they have filters at all – and yet these filters actually shape our reality, because they select from the mass of sound around us and bring to our attention only a small part of the total. Your reality is different from mine, because your filters are set differently to mine. Most people tragically assume that everyone else listens like they do, which causes untold misery and miscommunication.

In my third TED.com talk I suggest five skills for personal conscious listening, of which one is consciously choosing a "listening position" by playing with those filters; once we are aware of them, they become control surfaces that we can use to alter our attitude, adopting the position that's most appropriate and useful for any situation. For brands, it's vital to be aware of the prevalent filters of the target audience, and to send appropriately – in other words to empathise and understand the audience's listening position, and so speak into a well-defined listening.

1.2 We are losing our listening

It's not just noise that's causing us to lose our listening: there are many other factors. One is simply the ability to record what people say, which we've been able to do for several thousand years in the form of writing, and for the last hundred years or so in sound and then video. For most of man's history, knowledge was transmitted orally: if you missed it, you missed it. Now the premium on careful listening is much lower because we can usually press rewind and check it later.

Then there's diminished patience: most younger people want bullet points, not oratory; tracks, not albums; channel-hopping and multiple inputs instead of linear consumption from start to finish of one thing at a time. Along with this trend, our sensitivity is being eroded by media hyperbole and our whole system of relationships is radically changing because of social networking and technology: we are moving from narrow but deep relationship sets to wide but shallow, with many "friends" we have never actually heard at all – instead, we relate 140 characters at a time in text only[1]. There is little listening in the process of personal broadcasting.

1.3 Brands need to listen – right now!

Technology may be presenting challenges for us in our personal lives, but for brands it is creating great opportunities to move from traditional marketing, which was all about sending, to a new model that centres on listening. Some of the key transitions in that shift are shown below.

---

1   A great description of this phenomenon is Sherry Turkle's book Alone Together.

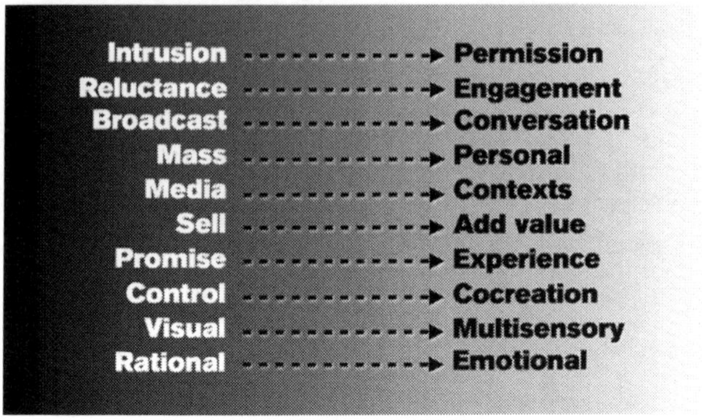

Intrusion	Permission
Reluctance	Engagement
Broadcast	Conversation
Mass	Personal
Media	Contexts
Sell	Add value
Promise	Experience
Control	Cocreation
Visual	Multisensory
Rational	Emotional

Figure 2. Old and new marketing paradigms

Incredibly, there are still brands who believe that broadcasting via mass media (AKA advertising) will be their primary marketing activity even 10 years from now. But the smart brands are listening with all the new ears the new technology affords them, whether that's a Facebook page, a whole department of brand Twitterati responding to any negative mention with a kind and witty word, or sophisticated keyword-hunting Internet robot hounds.

People change faster than organisations: most of us over 40 are amazed at the things our kids can do effortlessly where we still fumble and curse... and millions of these connected kids are becoming consumers every day. They expect to be listened to, and brands that fail to understand this can quickly experience being savaged by the wild dogs of peer review and trending outrage.

2. The Future of Retail Sound

For retailers, some of the most important words in the picture above are experience, emotional and multisensory. If physical retailers are to compete with the lure of Amazon and a couch, they need to create something worth coming out of the house for: not a chore, but a voyage of fun, engagement and enchantment, surprising and delighting their customers rather than boring, intimidating or overwhelming them.

2.1 Harrods

We at The Sound Agency are thrilled to have won the 2012 Gold Audio Branding Award for our work with Harrods, not least because we are passionate about creating a new paradigm for retail sound, which made it moving and inspiring for us to discover that our peers in the global audio branding industry share our vision and see that much-needed shift in retail sound as important too.

The work we showed comprised the dramatic soundscapes we have created for the new Toy Kingdom in the world's most famous store. A range of five complex, generative[2] soundscapes are delivered by our groundbreaking Ambifier™ players, each creating a magical sonic environment that reinforces the theme of the zone, from Big Top to the Enchanted Forest or the futuristic Odyssey. The power of super additivity (as passionately advocated by ABC2012 keynote speaker, Prof Charles Spence) is truly in evidence when soundscapes like these are carefully fashioned to express, amplify and harmonise with visual design.

This is just part of a huge project which started with a full sound audit of the store's 1 million square feet of retail space, identifying more than 200 audio zones and laying the foundation for a sound action plan that will see the whole store's sound transformed over the course of five years. The Toy Kingdom installation was the first, and already we have delivered two more departments, while at the time of writing working on three more. There will be challenges to overcome, not least in communicating the theory and practice to the 5,000 staff through a structured training programme so that people don't revert to bringing in their own music on an iPod! When we are done there will something like 30 hand-crafted music playlists plus around 20 generative soundscapes, all deployed on a state of the art sound system that's centrally controlled but responds to local changes in noise levels.

This is the future of retail sound. It is a long way from mindless music, and with good reason.

---

2 Generative sound is played live by computer, ever-changing and based on probabilistic algorithms. Most of ours are designed to be aural wallpaper: congruent, sustaining and effective without intending to be listened to consciously.

2.2 Mindless music is wrong for retail environments

As Professor Nancy Puccinelli said at ABC2012, many retailers are over-stimulating shoppers, with negative effects. A survey reported in the UK *Daily Mail* (November 4, 2011) found that 50% of shoppers leave stores because of the background music playing. This finding is a welcome anti-dote to a lot of often poorly-designed research suggesting that music is universally beneficial and so should be deployed absolutely everywhere. That is obviously not true, and yet the thesis sadly seems to have taken root in the minds of many retailers. I suspect that the explosion of mind-less music in public places is fuelled less by retailers' desire to improve the shopping environment than by the music industry's desperate search for new revenue streams. With sales of "product" collapsing, the music industry is left with just two revenue streams that are still growing: live shows, and royalties from public performance of recorded music. The moguls of music (and their acolytes in the royalty collection agencies) have seized onto background music with the desperate grasp of a drown-ing man on a piece of wreckage. It seems that their wish is to veneer with music every public space in the world – shops, malls, restaurants, cafés, outdoor spaces, buses, taxis, stations, airports, gyms, community build-ings.

In fact, veneering the world with music is pollution, not decoration. The *Daily Mail* survey reflects an earlier UK poll by *National Opinion Polls NOP* (sponsored in 1998 by Action on Hearing Loss), which found that roughly one third of people liked public background music, one third didn't care and one third hated it. Upsetting one third of your customers is a serious decision to take! The research that purports to show that we all love music everywhere is usually sponsored by the record companies or the licensing agencies, who have an obvious agenda, and much of it is methodologically unsound. In my experience, asking people what they think of music in a shop (or even worse, whether they like it) is useless – and again this point was validated by Nancy Puccinelli, who spent some time at ABC2012 talking about the unreliability of self-reported re-sponses to stimuli. The people who hate background music won't be in a shop to ask – they will already have gone somewhere else – so the sample is self-selecting and biased to start with. Then there's the fact that most people are unconscious of most background music until asked one of these questions, at which moment they start to listen consciously and crystallise an opinion instantly, based on the track currently playing.

Much more interesting than what people say is what they do. Do they leave the store sooner, or stay longer? Do they feel more or less stressed in the aural environment? Do they spend more or less money? Do they feel more or less affinity with the brand or the place? These questions can only be answered by testing different sound conditions and measuring these quantities or feelings without mentioning the sound at all. One survey I know of found three in five people turning around at the door of a shop with loud music and not entering at all. Researching those inside the shop would never have revealed this kind of damage. I suspect that the NOP survey is a fair picture of the real situation, and it shouldn't surprise us, for four reasons.

First, there is a basic conflict of interest at work. Almost all music is made to be listened to, not ignored. Intention is important with sound, so when this music is used as background sound there is a battle between the music's intention (to be listened to) and the intention of most of the people being exposed to it (shopping, talking, thinking and so on). Music is a very dense sound: it calls our attention to it, so it hinders cognition. We all know the feeling of rising stress when we try to think or talk with loud music playing. Most music is simply not fit for purpose as background sound when people are trying to process information. The visual equivalent of typical background music would be covering every inch of the walls in reproduction art. Nobody does that because it would be distracting, overwhelming and far too rich; plain walls are generally preferred because we don't have to pay them any attention. Exactly the same holds true for sound: it's just that we've become so used to suppressing our awareness of noise that we don't notice the craziness of wallpapering all our environments with music.

Second, most retail music is fast-paced pop, which is simply inappropriate for many stores. If you want to speed people up and reduce dwell time, play fast music (Milliman, 1988). Thus I can absolutely understand fast music in McDonald's – but not in Swarovski, Zara or T Mobile stores. Anyone selling high value or complex goods or services should be in the business of slowing people down and relaxing them, not speeding them up and generating stress hormones.

Third, music produces strong emotional responses through powerful associations. Two very similar people can have diametrically opposed reactions to a track simply because of its associations for them personally, and this is impossible to predict. Playing popular music is therefore liable to create potent and unpredictable responses, which is not very wise.

Finally, and related to the last point, most retail music is anodyne. Music programmers have to avoid the aural equivalent of over-strong flavours, not to mention any hint of sex, politics, violence or vulgarity (though profanity often slips through when urban music is not carefully listened to) – so we tend to end up with wall-to-wall ABBA or formula lounge music. Branded spaces should sound, as well as look, unique: you should be able to close your eyes and know where you are. If music is the same from shop to shop, it becomes meaningless to have it there at all. By contrast, strong music choices can be very effective. Abercrombie & Fitch use their loud and tightly selected music as a filter, and it works very well: they don't want me in there and I don't want me in there either! I dart in to pay for my daughter's choices when she's ready.

2.3 There are better solutions than music for retailers

Fortunately there are two great alternatives to music in retail spaces. Silence can be golden, especially if acoustics are well designed so that the space feels lovely to be in. In the pantheon of precious commodities for the 21st century, peace may well be the new time. Spaces that offer peace and quiet will, I suspect, do very well.

Where there is a need for aural wallpaper, then generative sound is a great option, as we are showing in Harrods and also in shopping malls across Europe. Played live by computer, always evolving, relatively free of associations and most of all designed to be ignored, this is the sonic equivalent of patterned wallpaper. It can incorporate natural sounds like birdsong or water to create ambiances of understated beauty, changing the mood and effect of a space dramatically.

2.4 The Golden Rules and the most common mistake

So let's not veneer the world with music. Let's honour it and listen to it, as it wants us to. Instead of abusing music, let's design sound in our public spaces just as carefully as we design shape, colour and lighting. Let's design experience, not just appearance. And where sound is concerned, here are my four Golden Rules.

1. Make it congruent with your brand or the values.
2. Make it appropriate for the situation.
3. Make sure it adds real value (and remember, silence is a sound, and can add great value just by giving people a rest from noise).
4. Test and test again, using continual research that measures how people feel and what they do in different soundscapes, without asking them what they think of the sound itself.

When you've got all that right, there's one more challenge. If you're going to create and play well-designed sound, don't fall at the last hurdle and skimp on the quality of your sound system – the most common mistake we come across. This is not a thing to be specified by quantity surveyors or IT/technical departments: you need to make sure that someone with good ears and a passion for your brand is involved.

Last and most important of all, train your staff to listen. This will pay dividends in every aspect of your business, from sales to customer care and team leadership. Make training in conscious listening skills a part of your induction, and of your ongoing training programme. The returns will be phenomenal, and we'll take one more step towards a listening world.

3. Conclusion

Brands need to listen. First, to the sounds they are making themselves. Second, to us, the audio branding industry, about the effects of the sound they are making and about what is possible for them. Third, and most important of all, to their customers.

I believe our industry has a responsibility to promote listening, not just among brand owners but in general. If nobody is listening, our work becomes rather pointless. But in a world where people are consciously listening, we can and will play a massively important role in helping to design sound that's effective, appropriate and often beautiful.

References

Milliman, R. E. (1982). Using background music to affect the behavior of super-market shoppers. Journal of Marketing, 46 (3), 86–91.

On Crossmodal Correspondences and the Future of Synaesthetic Marketing: Matching Music and Soundscapes to Tastes, Flavours, and Fragrances

Charles Spence

Crossmodal Research Laboratory, Oxford University

Key Words

multisensory design, synaesthetic marketing, crossmodal correspondences, music/soundscapes, taste/flavour

Abstract

For centuries, now, people have been excited by the possibility of meaningfully matching musical notes with tastes, flavours and perfumes (see Huxley, 1932; Huysmans, 1884; Piesse, 1862/1891, for early examples). However, until recently, it has never been clear whether such surprising crossmodal matches reflected anything more than the idle fancies of the creative minds who came up with them (a kind of idiosyncratic synaesthesia if you will). Over the last few years, though, cognitive neuroscientists have started to demonstrate that many of these crossmodal correspondences (sometimes called synaesthetic mappings) are actually remarkably robust (that is, shared by the majority of people within a community). As such, the opportunity arises to start scientifically developing music and soundscapes that correspond crossmodally to the tastes, flavours and fragrances of that which they are supposed to be associated

39

with. Perhaps unsurprisingly, sensory marketers are becoming increasingly excited by the possibilities associated with synaesthetic marketing.

1. Introduction

The last few years have seen something of an explosion of interest in the crossmodal mapping of music and soundscapes to tastes, flavours, aromas and even oral-somatosensory food textures (see Deroy et al., in press; Knöferle & Spence, 2012, for reviews). Of course, the idea itself certainly isn't new: For well over a century now, artists, novelists and perfumers have been writing about machines/devices that were capable of matching musical notes and instruments to specific tastes, flavours and perfumes (e.g., Huxley, 1932; Huysmans, 1884; Piesse, 1862/1891). Take, for example, the sensualist lead character Des Esseintes, in Huysmans's novel, "Á rebours" (often translated into English as "Against Nature"), who builds a "liqueur flavours keyboard" that allows him to play "on his palate a series of sensations analogous to those where music gratifies the ear". The taste of dry curaçao is, for Des Esseintes, very much like the "clarinet with its shrill, velvety note", while kummel corresponds to "the oboe, whose timbre is sonorous and nasal" (Huysmans, 1884/1926; pp. 59-61). Or take the scent organ that appears in Aldous Huxley's classic 1930's novel, "Brave New World". Elsewhere, Boris Vian apparently once described a "pianoctail" that he imagined would prepare drinks appropriate to the music that happened to be being played at the time (see This, 2009, p. 165).

However, for anyone thinking about the practicalities of matching music to tastes, flavours and/or fragrances in a meaningful (or, rather, generally accessible) manner, the worry has always been that the cross-sensory matches that have been described previously in (the) literature might reflect nothing more than the idiosyncratic matches of the authors concerned. Such crossmodal matches may, of course, have made sense to the writers themselves, but the intuition was that they would not feel right (or work) if tested empirically today. Indeed, many of the artists – novelists, painters, composers, poets – who have, over the years, experimented with the mixing of the senses in their work may even have been synaesthetes[1] (see Harrison, 2001). What is more, and complicating matters somewhat, several synaesthetes have been documented who have also experienced synaesthetic (i.e., illusory) tastes, aromas and/or flavours in response to hearing specific sounds, or vice versa. So, for example, one individual described a few years ago by Beeli, Esslen and Jäncke (2005) experienced specific tastes on hearing different musical tone intervals (e.g., a minor second gave rise to a sour taste on the tongue). Another synaesthete, S., the famous Russian mnemonist described by Luria (1968), experienced a wide variety of different aroma/flavour sensations in response to different sounds. For example, presented with a 50Hz tone (corresponding roughly to G1), he reported experiencing a taste that he likened to sweet-and-sour borscht. Meanwhile, listening to a tone of 3,000Hz (close to a G7), would give rise to an unpleasant taste that he likened to a briny pickle!

Now while such a synaesthetic mixing of the senses is undoubtedly interesting in its own right, I would argue that it is of little use/relevance when it comes to trying to decide which sounds, instruments, or musical parameters should, for example, be used to convey the flavour of citrus or vanilla (cf. Bronner et al., 2012). The reason being that synaesthesia is, by definition, idiosyncratic. What this means, in practice, is that (more often than not), each synaesthete has a different mapping between their senses. As such, it is nigh-on-impossible to extract any generalizations from such first-person synaesthetic reports that can, for example, be used by a composer or sonic designer who is trying to decide on the specific sound parameters that best match (or connote) a given taste, fragrance or flavour (e.g., when composing a jingle for a particular food product, say).

---

1 Synaesthetes are the rare individuals, though no one can agree quite how rare, who often tend to 'confuse their senses', most commonly seeing colours when they see or hear numbers of letters.

2. The Scientific Study of Crossmodal Correspondences

Now, the idea of scientifically ascertaining whether people do reliably match musical notes to particular tastes (which could be classed as a specific example of a crossmodal correspondence)2 was first pioneered by Kristian Holt-Hansen working in Denmark, some decades ago (see Holt-Hansen, 1968). It was he who first demonstrated that people (a group of around 10 participants) reliably chose a lower pitched tone as matching the taste of regular Carlsberg lager, while matching a some-what higher note to the taste/flavour of Carlsberg's Elephant beer (510-520 Hz vs. 640-670 Hz, respectively). Perhaps even more interesting was Holt-Hansen's subsequent finding that when the matching pitch, what he refered to as "the pitch of harmony", was played as a pulsed tone to people while they tasted the appropriate beer, people rated it as tasting better!

In a subsequent study, Holt-Hansen (1976) also noted that several of the participants reported having "extraordinary" experiences when the pitch of harmony was presented while tasting the matching beer. One participant, for example, reported that "My right hand with the glass of beer in it trembled so violently that I was suddenly afraid of dropping the glass. I felt as if I was floating in the air. The tone was intensified to such a degree that it sounded like a symphony orchestra and the room was filled with it. My jaws were moving in and out with the rhythm of the tone." Perhaps unsurprisingly (though in contrast to Holt-Hansen), no such extraordinary experiences were reported by the participants in a follow-up study published a few years later by Rudmin and Cappelli (1983). The participants in the latter study used a tone generator to pick a frequency that matched the flavour of one of several foods (Carlsberg beer, non-alcoholic beer, grapefruit juice, hard candy and dill pickle). It should be noted that while failing to demonstrate any extraordinary experiences, the researchers nevertheless did observe a significant effect of the foodstuff tasted on the pitch of the sound that was chosen.

---

2 Crossmodal correspondences have been defined as the often-surprising matching of features between the senses. So, for example, most people will match low pitched sounds with large objects that are situated low in space.

This early research has been pretty much forgotten about until the last few years when we have witnessed something of an explosion of interest in the crossmodal matching of music (and specific musical parameters) to tastes, flavours and fragrances. What is more, this interest has come both from individuals intuitively suggesting specific pieces of music to match everything from wine (see Spence, 2011b, for a review) through to beer (Brown, 2012 – The Pixies' Doolittle going particularly well with Duvel beer, apparently), through to cognitive neuroscientists working in many different countries now who have been systematically checking up on the reliability of particular crossmodal correspondences (e.g., see Mesz et al., 2011, 2012; Simner et al., 2010; Spence, 2011a, b; see Deroy et al., in press; and Knöferle & Spence, 2012, for recent reviews of this burgeoning literature).

This mixing of art and science – or, more precisely, musical compositions inspired (and/or constrained) by the scientific method has also proved interesting to the press (e.g., see Anon., 2012), thus bringing this particular area of crossmodal research to far wider public attention than might otherwise have been the case. What is more, a number of groups around the world have started to organize events involving everything from the repeating Holt-Hansen's classic study (that took place in Portugal recently) through to the matching of music to food, drink and/or fragrance (e.g., Wasselin, 2012); In the latter event, perfumers created scents that were diffused through the musicians and their audience. The musicians then played musical compositions inspired by the scents and improvised to that which they were smelling.

Below, I review a number of the latest exciting examples highlighting some of the various ways in which academic researchers and sonic design/branding practitioners have been working together recently in order to create music/soundscapes that not only match a particular food, beverage, or fragrance (based, in part, on the science of crossmodal correspondences), but which can also change (and ideally enhance) the consumer's experience of the product when experienced together with the music (though, it must be admitted that the contemporary research has never quite found the way to replicate the heady heights of the extraordinary experiences reported by certain of Holt-Hansen's participants back in the 1970s). As we will see below, a number of exciting and innovative new ideas and opportunities have recently started to emerge around the intelligent pairing of music designed to support/complement specific brand experiences. Digital technologies may also help to facilitate this "sensory explosion" of crossmodal sensory matching.

3. Music While You Eat?

In a recent collaboration between academia and sonic design practitioners (Crisinel et al., 2012), we conducted a series of experiments here at the Crossmodal Research Laboratory in Oxford in which participants were given pieces of bittersweet toffee (that had been prepared by The Fat Duck experimental research kitchen in Bray; see http://www.thefatduck.co.uk/) to taste while listening to one of two soundscapes developed by Condiment Junkie, a London-based sound design / sonic branding agency (see http://www.condimentjunkie.co.uk/). The soundscapes had been developed on the basis of prior laboratory research by Crisinel and Spence (2010a, b) higlighting the fact that people typically pick lower-pitched tones as matching (or corresponding crossmodally with) bitter tastes while reporting that higher-pitched sounds provide a better match for sweet tastes (e.g., see Knöferle & Spence, 2012, for a recent review).[3] Crisinel et al.'s results revealed that people's perception of the intensity of the bitterness and sweetness present in the toffee was modified sig-

---

3 The soundtracks were created using Logic 9 music production software. All of the sounds were presented in the key of F. The bitter soundtrack consisted of a blend of sinewave-based synthesised tones generated by the Sculpture Modeling synth and ES2 synth plug-ins, pitched at F2 (midi note 41) and C3 (midi note 48). These sounds were overlaid with a single trombone note played at F2, and a low frequency rumble created by passing a field recording of car traffic in a tunnel through a low pass filter. The main element of the sweet soundtrack was created from the Yamaha Grand piano plug-in, passed through Space Designer reverb unit set to 100% wet and 10% dry. The notes move in legato through the F scale pitched around C4 – C6 (midi notes 60 – 84). This sound was overlaid with a sinewave-based synthesised tone generated by the Sculpture Modelling synth plug-in in the same pitch, as well as abstractions of the piano sound created by resampling and reversing the sound several times. These soundscapes are available at: www.condimentjunkie.co.uk.

nificantly simply by varying the pitch of a soundtrack that was playing over headphones.[4]

A variant of "The bittersweet symphony" dish was recently featured on the menu at The House of Wolf (see http://houseofwolf.co.uk/), a newly-opened experiential dining restaurant in Islington, London. It was also featured as one of the dishes served at the 2012 annual Experimental Food Society banquet also held in London (http://www.experimentalfoodsociety.com). In these cases, when the diner reached the appropriate point on the tasting (or sensory) menu, they were provided with two phone numbers to call in order to listen to each of the soundtracks. I would argue that this is just one of the many ways in which digital technology will increasingly come to play a role at the dining table in the years to come (see Spence, in press; Spence & Piqueras-Fiszman, 2013).

Indeed, in the years to come, it would seem likely that a growing number of bars and restaurants will start to realize that the decision of which music they play is too important to be left to the manager's preferred iPod selection. Furthermore, in the future, it is to be anticipated that we will increasingly see technology being used to allow for the personalized delivery of music and/or soundscapes to individual tables (where, for example, a group of friends may be sharing a bottle of wine, say), or even to an individual diner or drinker (either through the use of headphones, as in "The sounds of the sea" seafood dish, served at The Fat Duck (see Spence, 2011a; Spence et al., 2011) or through the use of hyperdirectional loudspeakers.

In a similar vein, it is interesting to note how the last few years have seen the publication of a number of cookery books that have either been accompanied by a matching music CD (e.g., see Gagnaire & Gonzales, 2010), or else, in the case of the North American chef, Zakary Pelaccio, have included specific music recommendations to play while people prepare the dishes outlined in his book (Pelaccio, 2012).

---

4 Anecdotally, it seems as though this crossmodal effect of sound on taste works best when the soundscapes are presented over headphones rather than via external loudspeakers (perhaps because, in the former case, the sounds are localized within the head (i.e., from closer to where the taste/flavour of the toffee is experienced.)

4. Music While You Drink?

The synaesthetic matching of music with food and drink has not gone unnoticed by the sensory marketers and branding practitioners (Spence, 2012b). Indeed, some future forecasters may be wondering why it has taken so long for synaesthetic marketing to explode onto the market-place (e.g., Meehan, Samuel, & Abrahamson, 1998).[5] Over the last few years, a number of brands have started to explore the possibilities associated with matching music with their brands in a number of innovative ways. Back in 2011, for example, I was involved in a project together with Starbucks who were launching Starbucks Via, their instant coffee, into the UK marketplace. The company commissioned a piece of music (based on Crisinel & Spence, 2010b), that people at home could listen to, or download, from the Web in order to enhance their coffee drinking experience (see Spence, 2011a). The soundtrack had lots of low-pitched notes given the bitter taste of coffee.[6]

Now, as far as I am aware, no one has as yet conducted the appropriate empirical study in order to determine whether this particular hot beverage really does taste better (or at least different) if consumed while listening to this particular piece of music. However, what is undeniably the case is that the cognitive neuroscience approach to the matching of music to taste/flavour generated a huge amount of media interest around the brand, and hence this example of sensory marketing can be considered as a successful case studies of what a company can hope to achieve by matching music (or jingles) to their brands on the basis of the science of crossmodal correspondences.

Another exciting example that we have been working on recently relates to an interactive sensory app developed by Courvoisier (see Le Nez de Courvoisier App; http://courvoisier.com/uk/le-nez-de-courvoisier-app/).

---

5   As Meehan et al. (1998) put it: ""I don't think this banana is quite ripe ... it tastes a little triangular." Sound bizarre? Not in the new millennium, where sensory blending–tasting shapes, hearing colours, and seeing smells–will be anxiously expected."

6   And, of course, back in 1732, JS Bach wrote his Coffee Cantata. This secular piece of music, published in Leipzig, was written for soprano, tenor, bass solos and orchestra.

The flavour/aroma of Cognac is very complex, much like in the case of wine. The company concerned therefore developed a kit containing six small bottles, each containing one of the key notes found in their XO Imperial Cognac. The aromas included the smell of crème brûlée, ginger biscuits, candied orange, coffee, and iris flower. Next, a composer generated a series of short musical clips to match each of these aroma notes in the Cognac. The idea here was that consumers could listen individually to each of these musical pieces, and then once they had established (or, better still, guessed) the association between the three pieces of music and a given aroma, they could then listen to another musical composition in which each of the individual elements had been skilfully integrated into a single, more complex, piece of music (i.e., to in some sense match the complex interplay of aromas that you might find in a fine Cognac).

Now, here at the Crossmodal Research Laboratory in Oxford we have recently conducted a series of experiments in order to assess whether people can actually decode the intent, or aroma, that the composer had in mind when creating each of the musical pieces (see Crisinel et al., 2013). The participants in our study were presented with the three aromas (crème brûlée, ginger biscuits and candied orange) and three putatively matching (or corresponding) pieces of music, that were meant to be associated with each of them. The participants had to try and match each of the short musical pieces to the appropriate aroma. However, our results suggest that the composer has only been partially successful in this case. We are therefore currently working with sonic designers in order to try and develop a selection of musical excerpts that people more intuitively match to the aromas that can be found in Cognac.[7]

There are, however, two other things to note about the Courvoisier case. First, even if it turns out that people are unable to match the musical pieces to the specific aromas in a blind test that doesn't necessarily

---

7 To date, researchers have tended to be much better when trying to match music to tastes (e.g., sweet, sour, bitter, and salty; Mesz et al., 2011; Simner et al., 2010; see Knöferle & Spence, 2012, for a review) than to aromas or flavours. This may be, in part, because the range of basic tastes is much more tightly constrained than the range of possible aromas or flavours.

mean that this app should be judged a failure. For, having taught consumers a particular mapping between aroma and music, when the consumer subsequently drinks the Cognac while listening to one of the individual, or even the composite, piece of music, they may nevertheless still enjoy an enhanced multisensory brand experience.

5. The Music of Perfume

In our latest research, we have started to investigate the matching of sound to perfume. It is interesting to note how, for centuries, people have used musical terms in order to describe perfumes and fragrances. They talk of high and low (or bass) notes in a perfume, they talk of chords and harmonies (see Anon., 2012; Deroy et al., in press; Wasselin, 2012). Take, for example, the following quote from Septimus Piesse (1862/1891, p. 25): *"Scents, like sounds, appear to influence the olfactory nerve in certain definite degrees. There is, as it were, an octave of odours like an octave in music; certain odours coincide, like the keys of an instrument. Such as almond, heliotrope, vanilla, and orange-blossoms blend together, each producing different degrees of a nearly similar impression. Again, we have citron, lemon, orange-peel, and verbena, forming a higher octave of smells, which blend in a similar manner."*

Given the shared language of music and perfume, I would suggest that this may provide the framework for the establishment of a wide variety of crossmodal correspondences between music (or musical parameters) and the elements of perfume/fragrance. In our latest work with the world-famous perfumer, Roja Dove (see www.rdprgroup.com) we have demonstrated that it is possible to bring out either the "sweet" or "dry" notes in a variety of fragrances and perfumes by changing what it is that people are listening to (see Velasco et al., submitted).

6. Conclusions

While the scientific approach to establishing crossmodal correspondences between music (or musical parameters) tastes, flavours, and fragrances will certainly never supersede the more creative side of sound design/sonic branding, I would argue that it can nevertheless help constrain the creative process. Of course, sonic design can, and often has, been very successful without the need to resort to science (one might wonder here whether the most successful of sound designers simply intuit what the scientists typically need to study scientifically; cf. Koriat, 2008; though see Rudmin & Cappelli, 1983). That said, I would argue that having the scientific evidence concerning the relevant crossmodal correspondences for any given project/product to hand ought, at the very least, to give one a competitive advantage in the marketplace; not to mention the fact that savvy clients are increasingly asking (if not demanding) scientific proof that sonic design/branding works (and what better than the scientific method to provide such support)!

One other point to note here is that music and soundscapes are likely to be particularly effective when there are multiple tastes, flavours, or fragrances all competing (or vying for a person's attention). I would suggest that it is far easier to use music (or soundscapes) to bias a person's attention to one or other element of a complex mixture, than it is to create gustatory, olfactory, or flavour experiences out of thin air by sonic means alone. As has already been noted, it may be that sound might have more of an effect when presented over headphones than when presented from external loudspeakers (though further research is most definitely needed to support what, at present, is nothing more than a hunch). Finally, it is worth noting that while the approach described here has been very much based on matching the sonic attributes to the product or brand, the most successful of marketing and design strategies will undoubtedly need to appeal to all of a consumer's senses, not just the auditory.

References

Anon. (2012). Synaesthesia: Smells like Beethoven. The Economist, February 4, 74.

Beeli, G., Esslen, M., & Jäncke, L. (2005). When coloured sounds taste sweet. Nature, 434, 38.

Bronner, K., Frieler, K., Bruhn, H., Hirt, R., & Piper, D. (2012). What Is the Sound of Citrus? Research on the Correspondences between the Perception of Sound and Flavour. In: E. Cambouropoulos, C. Tsougras, P. Mavromatis, & K. Pastiadis (Eds.), Proceedings of the ICMPC – ESCOM 2012 Joint Conference, pp 42-48. Thessaloniki, Greece.

Brown, P. (2012). Ale, ale, rock and roll! Word Magazine, 28 March, 28-29.

Crisinel, A.-S., Cosser, S., King, S., Jones, R., Petrie, J. & Spence, C. (2012). A bittersweet symphony: Systematically modulating the taste of food by changing the sonic properties of the soundtrack playing in the background. Food Quality and Preference, 24, 201-204.

Crisinel, A.-S., Jacquier, C., Deroy, O. & Spence, C. (2013). Composing with crossmodal correspondences: Music and smells in concert. Chemosensory Perception, 6, 45-52.

Crisinel, A.-S. & Spence, C. (2010a). A sweet sound? Exploring implicit associations between basic tastes and pitch. Perception, 39, 417-425.

Crisinel, A.-S. & Spence, C. (2010b). As bitter as a trombone: Synesthetic correspondences in non-synesthetes between tastes and flavors and musical instruments and notes. Attention, Perception, & Psychophysics, 72, 1994-2002.

Crisinel, A.-S. & Spence, C. (2012a). A fruity note: Crossmodal associations between odors and musical notes. Chemical Senses, 37, 151-158.

Crisinel, A.-S. & Spence, C. (2012b). The impact of pleasantness ratings on crossmodal associations between food samples and musical notes. Food Quality and Preference, 24, 136-140.

Deroy, O., Crisinel, A.-S., & Spence, C. (in press). Crossmodal correspondences: Lessons from music and perfume. Psychonomic Bulletin & Review.

Gagnaire, P., & Gonzales, C. (2010). Bande originale. 175 Recettes & une heure de musique [Bande Originale. 175 recipes and an hour of music]. Paris: Flammarion.

Harrison, J. (2001). Synaesthesia: The strangest thing. Oxford: Oxford University Press.

Holt-Hansen, K. (1968). Taste and pitch. Perceptual and Motor Skills, 27, 59-68.

Holt-Hansen, K. (1976). Extraordinary experiences during cross-modal perception. Perceptual and Motor Skills, 43, 1023-1027.

Huxley, A. (1932). *Brave new world*. New York: Harper & Row.

Huysmans, J.-K. (1884/1926). *À rebours* [Against nature]. Paris: Charpentier.

Luria, A. R. (1968). *The mind of a mnemonist*. Cambridge, MA: Harvard University Press.

Knöferle, K. M. & Spence, C. (2012). Crossmodal correspondences between sounds and tastes. *Psychonomic Bulletin & Review*, 19, 992-1006.

Koriat, A. (2008). Subjective confidence in one's answers: The consensuality principle. *Journal of Experimental Psychology: Learning, Memory, and Cognition*, 34, 945-959.

Mesz, B., Sigman, M., & Trevisan, M. A. (2012). A composition algorithm based on crossmodal taste-music correspondences. *Frontiers in Human Neuroscience*, 6:71, 1-6.

Mesz, B., Trevisan, M., & Sigman, M. (2011). The taste of music. *Perception*, 40, 209-219.

Meehan, M., Samuel, L., & Abrahamson, V. (1998). *The future ain't what it used to be: The 40 cultural trends transforming your job, your life, your world*. New York: Riverhead Books.

Pelaccio, Z. (2012). *Eat with your hands*. New York: Ecco.

Piesse, C. H. (1862/1891). *Piesse's art of perfumery* (5th Ed.). London: Piesse and Lubin. Downloaded from http://www.gutenberg.org/files/16378/16378-h/16378-h.htm

Rudmin, F., & Cappelli, M. (1983). Tone-taste synesthesia: A replication. *Perceptual & Motor Skills*, 56, 118.

Simner, J., Cuskley, C., & Kirby, S. (2010). What sound does that taste? Crossmodal mapping across gustation and audition. *Perception*, 39, 553-569.

Spence, C. (2011a). Sound design: How understanding the brain of the consumer can enhance auditory and multisensory product/brand development. In K. Bronner, R. Hirt & C. Ringe (Eds.), *Audio Branding Academy Yearbook 2010/2011*, pp. 35-49. Baden-Baden, Germany: Nomos Verlag.

Spence, C. (2011b). Wine and music. *The World of Fine Wine*, 31, 96-104.

Spence, C. (2012a). Managing sensory expectations concerning products and brands: Capitalizing on the potential of sound and shape symbolism. *Journal of Consumer Psychology*, 22, 37-54.

Spence, C. (2012b). Synaesthetic marketing: Cross sensory selling that exploits unusual neural cues is finally coming of age. *The Wired World in 2013*, November, 104-107.

Spence, C. (2012c). Auditory contributions to flavour perception and feeding behaviour. *Physiology & Behaviour*, 107, 505-515.

Spence, C. (in press). Epilogue – Bringing technology to the dining table. To appear in J. H.-J. Choi, M. Foth, & G. Hearn (Eds.), *Eat, cook, grow: Mixing human-computer interactions with human-food interactions*. Cambridge, MA: MIT Press.

Spence, C., & Deroy, O. (in press). On why music changes what (we think) we taste. *i-Perception*.

Spence, C., & Piqueras-Fiszman, B. (2013). Technology at the dining table. *Flavour*, 2:16.

Spence, C., Shankar, M. U., & Blumenthal, H. (2011). 'Sound bites': Auditory contributions to the perception and consumption of food and drink. In F. Bacci & D. Melcher (Eds.), *Art and the senses*, pp. 207-238. Oxford: Oxford University Press.

This, H. (2009). *The science of the oven*. New York: Columbia University Press.

Velasco, C., Jones, R., King, S., Dove, R., Kellie, J., & Spence, C. (submitted). Smelling a sweet tune? Assessing the influence of soundscapes on the perception of fragrance. *Chemosensory Perception*.

Wasselin, C. (2012). Le concert des parfums [The concert of perfumes]. Downloaded from http://www.michel-godard.fr/download/PDF_INFO/Parfums_French.pdf on 05/01/2013.

Audio Branding Barometer 2012

Klaus Frieler

Audio Branding Academy

1. Introduction

As already in 2010 and 2011, the Audio Branding Academy conducted also in 2012 an online study devoted to the audio branding industry. Questions regarding business details and trend estimation were also included as well as items concerning sales arguments and the definition of terms. The same overall trends and basic facts as reported in 2010 and 2011 continue also in 2012. Audio Branding is a flourishing field – despite the prevailing world wide crises – and mostly run by rather small and young companies, showing continuously growing self-consciousness and self-esteem, thus sharpening its own meta-brand profile.

Results of this study were first presented at the ABC 2012, which took place in Oxford on December 11th, 2012.

2. Method & Sample

The study was carried out as an anonymous online survey during September and October 2012 using the free online survey tool oFb[1]. A comprehensive set of 145 audio branding agencies from all over the world was invited to participate. The final sample consisted of 33 agencies (response rate 22.7%) from 12 countries (Germany: 10, USA: 5, UK: 3, Bra-

---

1   http://www.soscisurvey.de

zil: 3, other countries & no answer: 11). 24 of the participants considered themselves as genuine audio branding agencies, the remaining 9 companies had other business orientations. 6 of the participating agencies are part of a company network.

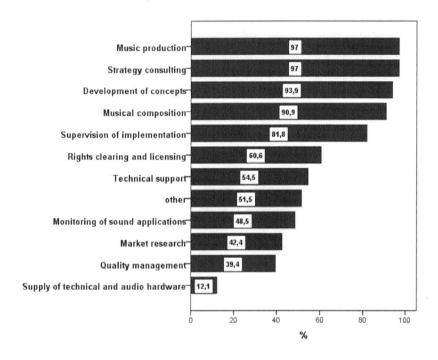

Figure 1. Services offered by the participants

The verdict from last year that Audio Branding is a "small and young company business" still holds in 2012: 13 respondents indicated to have only 1–3 employees in permanent position. 11 reported between 4 and 10 employees and only 9 companies stated to have more than 10 employees with one having more than 100 employees. Correspondingly, only 3 of the participating companies were founded before 1990, but 27 started business operation in the decade since 2001 (more than 80%). Nearly all companies offer music composition & production as well as strategic consulting / development of concepts, with shares of above 90% each (see **Figure 1**). Supplementary services, such as supervision, quality management, or market research are offered by about 50-60% of the respondents. The least common services (12.1%) are hard-ware related, e.g., supplying audio equipment.

3. Revenues and Clients

In 2011, the participating companies delivered most frequently audio logos (avg. 12.5% of all delivered items per company) and soundscapes (11.8%), followed by music on hold (8.9%) (cf. **Figure 2**). Music for commercials – last year's top item (Frieler, 2012) – was only produced 4.3% on average. These results are also rather different to 2010's results, where music on hold was the top deliverable (Köckritz, 2011).

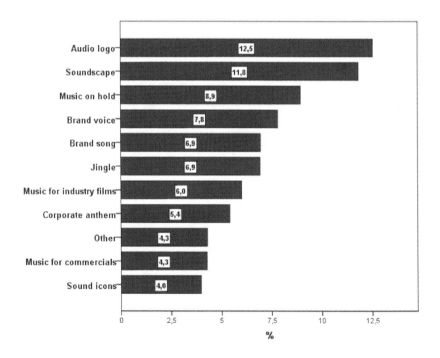

Figure 2. Median values of audio elements delivered by participants

The numbers of client projects is quite unevenly distributed. More than half of the 20 respondents indicated 10 or less client projects, two reported between 11 and 20, and five more than 20 projects. This result is reflected also in the distribution of budget sizes (cf. **Figure 3**).

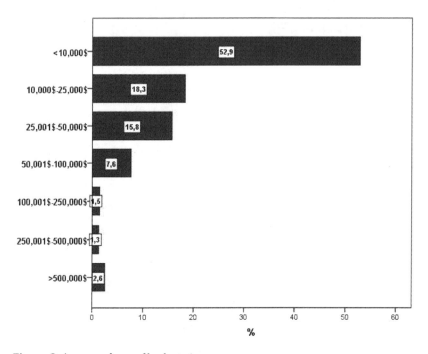

Figure 3. Average share of budget sizes

About 50% of all budgets are worth less than USD $10,000, and 87% of all budgets are smaller than USD $50,000. Only very few projects achieved a higher budget of over USD $50,000. The gross revenues of the participating companies are accordingly quite small, with median values of USD $170,000 for 2010 and USD $220,000 for 2011, but the relative change in revenue from 2010 to 2011 is rather promising (cf. **Figure 4**). While some companies experienced losses up to 50% and others achieved exceptionally high gains of up to 200%, the median of revenue change is about a considerable 32%. A comparison with the overall change of the sum revenues from the Audio Branding Barometers 2010 and 2011 of 10% and 12% (however calculated over the total sum not the of individual revenues), shows that the overall trend for the audio branding industry is still pointing upwards and might be even speeding up.

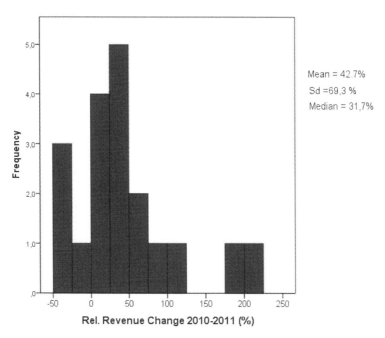

Figure 4. Revenue difference 2010-2011 (in USD $10,000)

Participants were also asked to estimate the share of client industries among their customers, according to number of projects (**Figure 5**) and to revenue (**Figure 6**). The most important clients – with around 30% share – are retailers and wholesaler, counted by approx. 50% of all respondents among their customers. Second most important was the construction industry with about 20% revenue share.

On the other hand, the largest numbers of projects were issued by Finance, Automotive, Health Care, Food, Beverage & Tobacco as well as Retailers and Telecommunications.

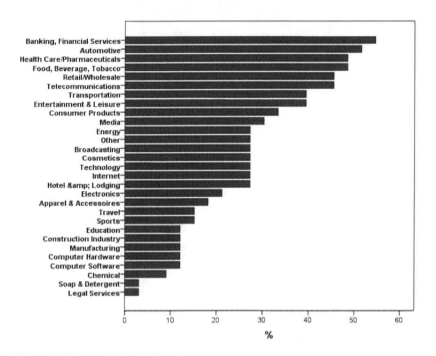

Figure 5. Shares of client industries

Obviously, there are rather large differences in budget sizes with respect to client industry. Comparing this with the numbers from last year and the year before last year – which showed quite a different structure – it can be supposed that these results depend heavily on the sample at hand. No conclusive statement can yet be made, which industries are more open to audio branding services.

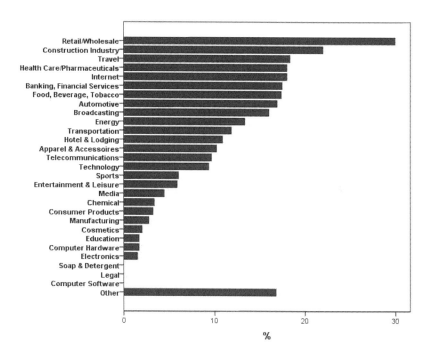

Figure 6. Average budget share of client industries

Finally, the participants were asked for the average daily fees for different business positions. The resulting boxplots are shown in **Figure 7**. The median values for Managing and Creative Directors are USD $1,500 per day, followed by Senior Managers with USD $1,250, Junior Managers with USD $800 and Assistants with USD $600. The near equal distribution for Managing and Creative Director might be due to the fact that in our sample of rather small companies these positions might be more often than not held by a single person.

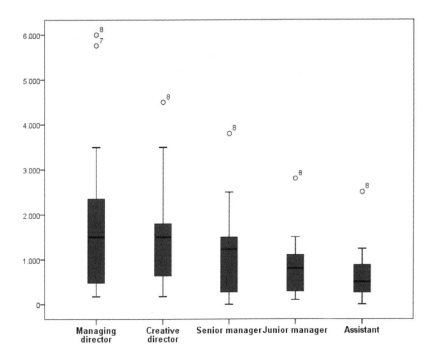

Figure 7. Boxplot of daily rates

4. New Business

Participants were also asked about new business acquisitions and pitches. The answers to the two different categories of general business projects and audio branding projects yielded slightly inconsistent data due to different subsets of participants answering these questions.

Only five respondents reported more than 10 new audio branding projects in 2011, whereas 21 companies achieved 10 or less and one did not start any new project. With regard to the totality of new business projects, 11 of the participants reported 4–10 successful business acquisitions, nine indicated 1–3, and three respondents had none. Only three participants reported more than 10 new business projects. Asked for competitive pitches in 2011, nine companies reported no competitive pitch at all, while the majority of 15 participants had up to 10 pitches. Only two companies achieved more than 20 pitches. An average fee for competitive pitches between USD $1,000 and USD $4,000 was reported by four agencies, four indicated USD $5,000 on average. The majority of seven respondents had only pitches without fees. On the other hand, four participants achieved fees beyond USD $5,000.

5. Trends

As in last year's surveys, participants were asked to estimate the business development for last and next year. The majority of 10 respondents saw a slight increase in the audio branding market from 2011 to 2012, with four indicating even a strong increase. Seven participants saw no change while two reported a slight decrease. No one reported a strong decrease. Respondents are mildly optimistic for the upcoming year. 28 agencies expect a slight (21 answer) or a strong increase (7 answers), and again, no one expects a strong decline. Only two foresee a slight decrease while three assume no change at all. Furthermore, participants were asked to judge the business perspectives in 10 years. Here, respondents are strongly optimistic, as 31 expect a slight (2 answers) and the overwhelming majority even a strong increase (21 answers). This is absolutely in line with last year's results and proves the continuing optimistic mood of the Audio Branding industry.

6. Terminology

Also this year, questions concerning the still debated issue of terminology were included in the survey. No final naming conventions have been established in the community yet, but there are some interesting tendencies of language resp. country dependent preferences (cf. below).

The request to name the acoustic equivalent to "Visual Branding" was answered with "Sound Branding" by 15 participants, "Audio Branding" coming second with nine answers, followed by "Sonic Branding" with seven answers. The rest gave different answers or no answer at all. The same rank order of specifiers was obtained for the acoustic equivalent of "Visual Logo": "Sound Logo" (15), "Audio Logo" (8), and "Sonic Logo" (4), other answers (6). It seems that this year "Sound" was the most preferred analogue to "Visual", opposed to last year's "Audio", but similar to the results of 2010. This made us wonder, if naming preferences really do oscillate with time – which seems unlikely – or if this effect might be a result of the particular set of respondents. In 2012 and 2010 the majority of participants came from Germany, whereas in 2011 the majority was from the US and the UK. To check for this hypotheses, we pooled the data for the "Visual Logo" and "Visual Branding" analogues from 2011 and 2012, and classified the participants in four different language categories according to their origin: British English (UK, Australia, South Africa, India), American English (USA), German (Germany, Austria, Switzerland) and "Other". This resulted in a total of 60 cases. Since there is an unknown intersection of respondents who participated in both studies, no proper statistical test could be carried out. Furthermore, the language classification was made quite ad-hoc and might not be fully correct, since the language had to be guessed from the country of origin of the respondent.

Nevertheless, the results show clear tendencies. First, participants nearly always use the same prefix for the different terms, hence, we will focus on the "Visual Branding" analogues for the discussion (cf. Tab. 1). Secondly, a preference for "Sound Branding" can be found for the German-speaking (9 out of 18), the British-speaking (4 out of 13) as well as for the "Other" participants (10 out of 18). None of the American-speaking companies employ the term "Sound Branding" (nor "Sound Logo") whatsoever. American agencies prefer almost exclusively "Audio Branding" (9/11), followed by "Sonic Branding" (2/11). The German-speaking companies and companies from the "Other" languages show a quite similar usage pattern. Following "Sound Branding", the term "Audio Branding" is used roughly half of the time as "Sound Branding" (5/18 for both). None of the German-speaking respondents and only one from the "Other" respondents uses the term "Sonic Branding". This might be explained by the fact that – at least for the German speakers – "Sonic" and the German equivalent "Sonisch" have no wide-spread use in German-speaking countries, whereas "Audio" and "Sound" are well-known words. The British-speaking agencies are the most diverse in their terminology, since "Sonic Branding" is used by the same share (4/13) as "Sound Branding", closely followed by "Audio Branding" with 3 out of 13 answers. To sum up, the data show a clear dependency of terminology on the country of origin of the companies.

	German	British	American	Other	Total
Sound Branding	9	4	0	10	23
Audio Branding	5	3	9	5	22
Sonic Branding	0	4	2	1	7
Acoustic Branding	2	1	0	0	3
Other	2	1	0	2	5
Total	18	13	11	18	60

Table 1. Cross-table of term usage for the "Visual Branding" analogue according to language of participants pooled from the 2011 and 2012 data sets. (German: Germany, Austria and Switzerland; British: UK; Australia, South Africa, India, American: USA, Other: All others).

7. Definition of Audio Branding

In a last section of the survey, participants were asked to provide a definition of Audio Branding. A total of 32 definitions of varying length and depth were given. The diversity of key points was naturally wide, but a trend to focus on branding aspects can be stated. Moreover, nearly no one used any reference to the visual domain, whereas this was done quite frequently last year.

A qualitative analysis of the definitions revealed the following most important key elements:

- Often explicit explanations with reference to branding ("Translating brand values into sound") were given.
- Many defined Audio Branding as "an integral part of holistic branding" or as "brand enhancement".

- Accordingly, "brand consistency" and "strategic orientation" were often emphasized.
- Some gave definitions in more general terms ("Sound communication") without explicit reference to branding.
- Generally, most participants conceived Audio Branding as a process rather than as products or deliverables.
- Quite a few touched on the "Multisensorial" and "Across touchpoints" aspects of Audio Branding.

Most of these aspects were neatly captured in this year's catch phrase given by one respondent: "Audio branding is the real 'bass' to (sic) the brand".

8. Sales Arguments

The participants were also prompted to state up to five sales arguments. A total of 136 arguments were obtained, naturally showing a great variety. By qualitative data analysis using manual clustering and classification, the following seven categories can be identified:

1. **Branding** (63 instances). The main line of this class of arguments is that audio can significantly enhance the branding process. This rather large class comprises several subcategories:
   a. **Holistic branding** ("Make your values heard"), 24 instances;
   b. **Differentiation** ("Corporate Sound helps brand uniqueness"), 12 instances;
   c. **Multisensory Aspects** ("Your brand is experienced in five senses, not one"), 6 instances;
   d. **Identity** ("Music/sound clarifies your brand identity"), 6 instances;
   e. **Recognition**, 7 instances;
   f. **Recall** ("Strengthens memory and brand recall"), 4 instances;

g. **Strategic Orientation** ("Sound should be born from a strategy that makes the brand really unique"), 4 instances.

2. **Emotional connection** (19 cases). In this class of arguments the unique power of music for inducing and communicating emotions is the main aspect. Emotion is also often linked to consumer engagement. Two subcategories can be differentiated:

   a. **Emotional connection** ("Sound emotionally connects with your customers"), 12 instances.

   b. **Engagement** ("Sound effectively builds engagement with consumers"), 7 instances.

3. **Profit** (17 instances). Of course, one of the most classical sales arguments is used as well: Audio branding increases the profit of the customer. Two main aspects can be distinguished:

   a. **Return on Investment** ("Good sound increases sales"), 10 instances;

   b. **Efficiency** ("Costs little and makes you save a lot"), 7 instances.

4. **Audio Specific** (4 instances). This class comprised arguments related to unique and specific properties of the audio channel (e.g., "People can stop seeing, but not stop hearing").

5. **Touchpoints** (4 instances). This class of arguments emphasizes the importance of consistency across touch points and is thus related to holistic branding as well.

6. **Trendy** (3 instances). These arguments play on the "trendiness" and "newness" of audio branding.

7. **Miscellaneous** (18 instances). Sales argument are diverse and can be quite creative, hence a rather large class of miscellaneous arguments emerged, ranging from "Scientific, research driven", over "Story telling" to "It's magic" or simply "It's relevant".

9. Conclusion

The results of this year's Audio Branding Barometer clearly indicate that the business is thriving, despite international finance and economical crises. Revenues are still growing, and thus optimism is the prevalent attitude. Moreover, the Audio Branding definitions and given sale arguments indicate a growing self-esteem and self-consciousness of Audio Branding as an important subfield of general branding which is becoming more and more well-known among potential customers.

References

Frieler, Klaus (2012). Audio Branding Barometer 2011. In K. Bronner, R. Hirt & C. Ringe (Eds.), Audio Branding Yearbook 2011/2012 (pp. 39-56), Baden-Baden: Nomos.

Köckritz, Jens. (2011). Audio Branding Barometer 2010. In: K. Bronner, R. Hirt & C. Ringe (Eds.), Audio Branding Yearbook 2010/2011 (pp. 55-65), Baden-Baden: Nomos, Edition Fischer.

Audio Branding Award 2012

In 2012, the Audio Branding Academy announced the second Audio Branding Award, to be presented to the single most outstanding case study showcased at the 2012 Audio Branding Congress. Seven case studies in the field of audio branding were nominated by a jury of audio branding experts. These cases were presented at the 2012 Congress by a representative from the agency or company. The winner was chosen by popular vote of the Congress participants – see also article *Audio Branding Congress 2012 Summary*.

Branded Globally – Relevant Locally

Henry Daw

Principal Sound Designer at Nokia

1. Global to Local

If you think of some of the big Global Brands, an audio identity may or may not come to mind, but as we see more and more global companies focusing efforts on developing their audio identities, the tendency is to follow audio branding and music trends emanating from Europe and the West.

Of course, we live in a world that is incredibly diverse, clearly evidenced by the vast differences in music culture. There is simply an amazing array of exciting, vibrant, and evocative music around the world, which can be very powerful and symbolic to someone based on where they come from. And so a question that needs to be asked by every global brand is: How can we be locally relevant through audio?

1.1 Marketing

The obvious approach to being locally relevant comes through local marketing. This can be as simple as running a localized marketing campaign, using accompanying music that would be appealing for people within that country or region. A global brand can also associate themselves with local artists, as a way of trying to connect. But if we move away from marketing, which within our field as in-house sound designers is often completely outside our control, it gets to be a bit more challenging.

1.2 Product sound

For Product Sound we are of course talking about mobile devices. Let's consider this spherical shape (shown in **Figure 1**) to represent Nokia's audio brand through devices. The inner core is of course the default ringtone (the Nokia Tune), which strongly influences also the start-up tone, as well as the default alerts (sms, calendar, clock and email). The primary objective of any global brand when it comes to audio branding should be to establish an audio brand core, an audio identity. It can be argued that only then can a company effectively strategize for localization with audio.

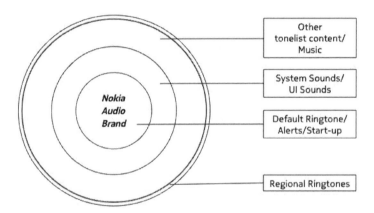

Figure 1. Nokia Audio Brand Sphere

Other sounds that sit just outside of this inner core also form an important part of the audio brand. We have all the various system sounds on the devices, such as battery low, keypad sounds, etc. Even further out from the core, you have all the additional ringtones and music tracks that come pre-loaded onto the devices. These ringtones and music tracks should really reflect Nokia's brand voice, whilst offering a varying selection for everyone. Of course it's a fine line that needs to be determined - reflect the Nokia brand but also offer a selection that caters for most user tastes.

1.3 Flexible audio brand

Of course, if you maintain a consistent audio brand, it doesn't necessarily mean the brand has to remain completely rigid. There should still be some flexibility within an audio brand after it's been established. This could allow for co-creativity (for example crowdsourcing) or localization. This is the area Nokia targets for localization: keeping the inner core of the audio brand true, whilst offering regional ringtones that would be targeted to people living outside of Europe and the West, further expressing the Nokia brand through audio.

2. Regional Ringtones

Nokia's commitment to providing locally relevant content has seen them offer regional ringtones for over 10 years, stretching all the way back to the time when I joined Nokia in 2002.

2.1 The early MIDI days (2002–)

During these times we were sourcing original MIDI ringtones from companies based in South East Asia. The ringtones were targeted separately for China, and also countries within South East Asia such as Singapore, Malaysia, Philippines, Thailand, Indonesia and Vietnam. Our team was making final judgment in terms of the quality of the ringtones, but by sourcing locally, the content relevance should be more appropriate, compared to what it could be if we were to design them in-house. The Chinese and South East Asia MIDI ringtones continued for a few years, until we more or less ceased MIDI production. This coincided with the time when practically all our devices were able to play audio formats.

2.2 First audio offering (2007–)

After MIDI production ceased, it was a bit more complex to get the level of quality we required for our regional ringtones. After much searching and assistance from local Nokia Sourcing teams, we found a group of companies who we felt matched the standards required, offering locally relevant ringtones whilst being able to accurately reflect our brand. At this time we would also be extending the scope of the regional ringtones, beyond China and South East Asia & Pacific, to include also India, Middle East & Africa and Latin America.

After much contemplation and research, during which time my eyes would be opened to the damaging consequences of commercialization around the world, and the effect on traditional local music cultures, I determined that our regional ringtones would not necessarily strictly follow local music trends (which commonly consists of Western style pop music with regional lyrics), but more so celebrate local music culture, based predominantly on traditional/folk styles.

My main philosophy behind the creation of the extensive regional ringtone offering was to try and create a good impression with someone by providing music that reflects their culture (i.e. someone living in China). Whether that person chooses to use that ringtone or not wasn't really so important, and this draws us away from the dangerous area of trying to keep up with local music trends, or being too focused on the younger aged-segments.

2.3 Present time

We would acquire a lot of content during the years 2007 - 2010, enabling us to vary the product selections each year, until we needed to renew everything again. This is when we decided to use crowdsourcing as a means to acquire new and locally relevant regional ringtones.

3. User Testing and Research

Before introducing our latest crowdsourcing project, I feel it's important to highlight some of the testing we do around our regional ringtones. This is an especially important aspect for our small team, which is based solely in London and Helsinki.

3.1 Quantitative studies

Our primary method for user testing our regional content is through quantitative user studies, within the regions the ringtones were designed for. From the studies we'll gather lots of useful data, including:

- **Popularity ratings**
- **Regional vs Global** (global ringtones includes all the ringtones pre-loaded to every region, typically based on Western styles)
- **Regional music preferences**
- **Ringtone usage habits**

All the information we can gather from these studies, can then aid our selections for the regional ringtone offerings. As we have typically done, this has traditionally consisted of a yearly selection of five ringtones for each region or country that we are targeting.

3.2 In-house research

Aside from the large user studies, it's important that we also continually try to teach ourselves within Nokia's Sound Team. This isn't really work, as of course we all love music, but we need to try and educate ourselves about the different music cultures around the world – the history, and where they are today. Of course, it's also about listening to lots of music, music that we perhaps might not normally listen to, music that you have to really find. We can also learn a lot by just talking with local people. So not by just reading books or listening to music, but by speaking with people who are from a particular region, and who are experts in the local music.

4. Crowdsourcing

Our most recent initiative to acquire locally relevant content has seen us turn to the exciting concept of crowdsourcing, an empowering practise which is seen as very relevant today. It is becoming almost a requisite that companies open up and connect with fans of their brand, and audio branding can certainly play a part in this.

Branded Globally – Relevant Locally

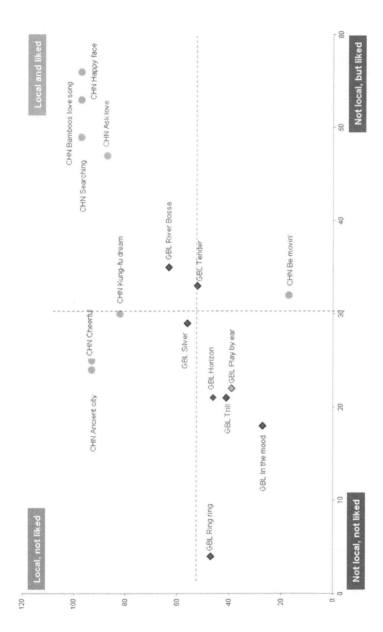

Figure 2. User Testing Example 1: Testing of China Regional Ringtones against our Global Ringtones

	Pop	Classical	Rock	Movie ST	Dance	Country	Electronic	Blues	Hip-Hop	Jazz	Soul/R&B	Folk	Alternative	World	Latin	Reggae	Children	Bollywood
UK	36%	28%	42%	22%	14%	18%	8%	10%	8%	11%	20%	8%	12%	3%	3%	7%	3%	1%
US		21%	47%		11%	36%	7%	12%	12%	14%	13%	6%	11%	3%	4%	6%	4%	1%
Brazil	31%		40%	32%	26%	10%	26%	12%	14%	9%	9%		10%	11%	9%	10%	5%	2%
Russia	31%	33%	31%	24%	34%		19%	20%	7%	14%	7%		5%	10%	9%	5%	4%	1%
China	53%	34%		36%	19%	21%	15%	10%	7%			21%	4%	4%	3%		5%	3%
Egypt	77%	48%							8%			9%		6%	3%		4%	0%
India	30%		18%	36%	16%		5%		9%		4%	15%		2%	3%		14%	30%

Significantly higher mentions

Significantly lower mentions

Figure 3. User Testing Example 2: Regional Music Preferences

4.1 Nokia Tune Remake

Of course most of you will know that Nokia has already made a major foray into the concept of audio crowdsourcing. Using the ever-growing Audiodraft platform, the Nokia Tune Remake was a remarkable success back in October 2011 (with admittedly a few bumps along the way!). This crowdsourcing contest really highlighted the benefits of opening up your audio brand to communities, whilst keeping the core true. The Nokia Tune Remake contest also highlighted the vast global user base that Nokia has, with entries coming from over 150 different countries. There were also many entries that had a local flavor, especially Chinese, Latin, Arabic and Indian.

4.2 Regional Ringtones, Designed By You

The Nokia Tune Remake laid an excellent foundation for our latest foray into Crowdsourcing; "Regional Ringtones, Designed By You". The contest was about Nokia reaching out and asking you to create ringtones that reflect and celebrate your local music cultures and styles. We wanted people to help us spread the exciting diversity of music around the world and support our firm belief in a thriving local music culture.

Again, we used the Audiodraft platform. We had five contests running concurrently, for four weeks. We had a contest each for the five different regions or countries that correspond with Nokia's sales areas outside of Europe and the West; China, India, South East Asia & Pacific, Middle East & Africa and Latin America. We were looking to select 5 winning ringtones for each region, each receiving $1500 cash prize, equating to a prize fund of $37,500. In addition, the winning ringtones would form our regional ringtone offering, sitting in the phone as pre-load for the region they were designed for.

4.3 Community spirit

The contest was set up a bit differently than the Nokia Tune contest – As well as the contest-holder's ratings, we would also be encouraging the Audiodraft community to rate the content. The community ratings would provide insights for when it comes to selecting the winners. The community spirit was excellent throughout with everyone grateful for the opportunity that Nokia were giving him or her, and also very grateful for all the feedback I was giving back.

4.4 Excellent PR

It was key to get the PR spot on. However, it's important to recognize that this was a completely different contest compared to the Nokia Tune Remake. For the Regional Ringtones contest we were looking for original compositions. Previously, the Nokia Tune melody was provided for the designers, and this led to thousands of entries, with a very widespread degree of quality. With the Regional Ringtones, it was about really connecting with the Audiodraft community, getting them to reflect local music whilst learning how to produce the perfect ringtone for functionality and appropriateness.

We had stories running through Nokia BrandBook blog, and Nokia Conversations, including localized versions of Nokia Conversations for China and Latin America. We were really trying to get the message out to everyone, including vitally, the people within the contest regions.

4.5 The stats

There were a total of 1500 entries pretty evenly spread across all five contests, which was a very pleasing outcome. It certainly kept me very busy for four weeks – I was attempting to give personal feedback for every single entry. There were also a total of 474 sound designers, which tells you that several people were submitting far more than one entry. Not only that, it was very common for people to submit to more than one contest. An interesting stat is that there were 30% of people entering from within India. To me, this shows a passion for not only Indian music culture, but also a passion for the Nokia brand.

4.6 The winners!

You can also preview all 25 winning entries in full from the Audiodraft website. In addition, they have been made available for everyone to freely download from the Nokia Store. The Nokia Store has been valuable for getting our ringtones out to everyone. To this point we have had over 40 million downloads of our ringtones – and since all 25 regional ringtones were put up 3 months ago, we've had over 3 million downloads.

4.7 Final word

"Regional Ringtones, Designed By You" has unquestionably been a very successful crowdsourcing campaign, which has yielded high quality results, both in terms of content and communiucation. Nokia prides itself on being locally relevant, on many different levels, and hopefully we have demonstrated to you, through this case study, how you can effectively take the principals of audio branding and apply them to not only localization, but also crowdsourcing. Audio crowdsourcing may not suit every company, but it has certainly worked well for Nokia, and there's no doubt that we will build on the success of the Nokia Tune and Regional Ringtones contests, whilst continually looking for new and innovative ways to enhance Nokia's audio brand.

List of Participating Agencies:

Crowdsourcing Campaigns:
Audiodraft (Finland)

User Research:
GFK (UK)
Foviance (UK)

Regional Ringtone Production:
6Du (China)
Hungama (China)
TRSS (China)
Qanawat (UAE)
FF Productions (India)
Soundbuzz (Singapore)
Snakeweed (Singapore)
Faith (Japan)
Music Airport (Japan)

The Globosat Case

Natalia Lannes

Gomus

1. Music Demand

The demands for audio and music of a television channel are never-ending. Besides having a constant need for audio-visual material, all audio must match the visual story and vice-versa. In addition, every communication a brand sends out should be congruent to its identity.

Globosat is a Brazilian pay-TV network. It is the largest pay-TV in Latin America and its audience numbers about 35.7 million viewers (PTS 179 - Sept./Oct. 2011). It has a total of 36 channels that cater specifically segmented markets, from kids, women to adults and teenagers. Besides producing many of its shows in-house, Globosat builds each channel's identity through the use of audio-visual material to mirror the specific audience they aim to reach. With the number of pay-tv viewers in Brazil, which grew about 24% in 2012 (*Hábitos & Consumo 15a ed.*), Globosat's challenge is to maintain its leading position, continue producing top quality shows, while being true to each channel identity.

Gomus' task was to help the audio choice process, as well as to bring out each channel's identity – the brand identity – through music, whenever it was being used.

1.1 Where did Globosat stand?

Each of the 36 channels is carefully designed to communicate directly with a specific demographic. Although the visual identities of channels have strong guidelines, Globosat had no guidelines regarding the use of audio in its communication. The method for choosing music was non-official, often relying on personal choice. Moreover, licensing music was a long and sometimes unrealistic process, considering the dynamics of in-house production. On top, Globosat had a library of more than 50,000 white tracks that they had bought over the years which were unorganized and unclassified – making the music choice process difficult. Taking all into consideration, Globosat needed guidelines defining each channel's audio identity, as well as an official and efficient method for picking out the best music available for a specific piece.

2. Deliverables

Gomus pioneered this project with Globosat's top 3 channels: GNT (women's variety), SporTV (sports) and Multishow (youth entertainment).

2.1 The Audio Brand Guide

The Audio Brand Guide (ABG) is a comprehensive booklet created by Gomus directing the use of audio in each one of the channels' communications. Besides defining and explaining the audio identity of each channel, the guide contains information about musical elements that should be used in order to convey that identity, and it explains step-by-step how to conduct a search in the software provided.

Figure 1. ABGs

2.2 The White Tracks

Over the years, the network had acquired a number of *white tracks* from various libraries for the channels. With over 50,000 tracks to choose from, the process of finding the right track for the right piece became slow, and often, good tracks were difficult to be found. Gomus listened and classified each one of those tracks according to the channels. The process of filtering white tracks began with an overall quality filter when listening to each one of the tracks. In order to maintain the quality, our team discarded every single audio file that had bad quality or sounded aged. Secondly, the tracks were classified according to the identity of each channel – GNT, SporTV and Multishow. Lastly they were classified within playlists to make it even easier to find the correct track.

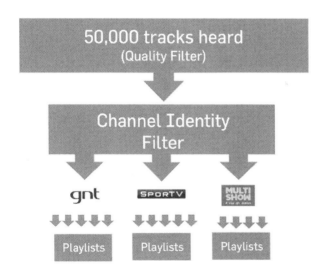

Figure 2. White Tracks Filtering Process

2.3 Licensing Original Tracks

Besides using white tracks from their library, Globosat often needs original tracks to synch with pieces. On a regular basis, Gomus recommends tracks to be used that are congruent to each channel's demands, needs and identity. Because often the process of licensing an original track can be long, every recommendation given to the network is accompanied by its licensing information – contacts for both master and publishing in national territory. This makes it possible for each channel to license tracks on a timely manner, and have an original track on air meanwhile the track is still fresh.

3. Search Engine Software

With all white tracks filtered and more original tracks recommended, the last step of the process was to find a quick way to store and search for music. Gomus created a software that became available to every employee at Globosat working in the audio-visual area. This software was installed in their computers, containing all the music available per channel, so that people that work for specific channels can only access music classified and filtered for them. The software takes inputs such as playlists, genres and mood (positive vs. introspective & calm vs. energetic). The user can find the right track for the right occasion within seconds, and have it available for use in no time.

Figure 3. Search Software

4. Results

The result of this project is a certified internal optimization when searching for the right track. It became less subjective and individual and more directed, planned and supervised. White tracks already purchased by Globosat also became easier to find, with high quality standards. For the first time, the audio identity of each channel was defined and documented, pairing its standards to the visual identity the channels already had. In addition, the channels gained agility and efficiency when licensing tracks for synch.

References

Guerra, Guto (2013). Music Branding: Qual é o som da sua marca?. Ed. Campus Elsevier. Rio de Janeiro. 20

PTS 179 – Sept. / Oct. 2011 http://canaisglobosat.globo.com/

Hábitos & Consumo 15a edição http://globosatcomercial.globo.com/habitos_consumo

DKSH Audio Branding

Johannes Pauen, Alexander Wodrich
kleiner und bold (Berlin)

1. DKSH

Switzerland-based DKSH is the leading Market Expansion Services Group with a focus on Asia. They help companies that are looking for a reliable outsourcing partner to help expand their business in new or existing markets. As its slogan says: Think Asia – Think DKSH. The company has been in business for almost 150 years and is one of Switzerland's Top 20 enterprises (www.dksh.com).

Figure 1. DKSH Logo

2. Strategic Goal

In 2011, after DKSH's lead agency for branding, kleiner und bold (Berlin), completed the corporate identity and design implementation, the company wanted to enhance their brand presentation by adding a brand sound – one that reflects both its Swiss and Asian heritage.

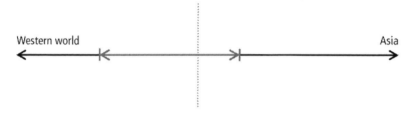

Figure 2. Positioning of the DKSH brand sound

3. Asia and Switzerland

Research conducted into the listening habits in Asian markets clearly showed that they are very noisy places. So in the audio branding workshop, DKSH decided to go for a sound with a somewhat introverted intensity, one with depth and distinct from its extroverted, loud competitors.

While looking for a lead instrument for the DKSH brand sound, various Asian and Swiss instruments were analyzed while always posing the question of whether or not it would be accepted as a general Asian sound in all Asian markets. A typical sound from a specific Asian country was not desired.

For that reason, an Asian musicologist was consulted regularly, providing professional feedback on the "Asian perception" of certain musical ideas. Furthermore, an advisory board, consisting of 15 international DKSH marketing team members from different markets, was implemented. Milestone presentations were held during global web-conferences.

4. The DKSH Audio Elements

The "hammered dulcimer" was finally chosen to be the lead instrument for the DKSH brand sound. It is a traditional Swiss instrument that sounds similar to typical Asian string instruments, yet it does not highlight a certain Asian country.

Figure 3. The lead instrument of the DKSH brand sound: the hammered Dulcimer

Delicately mixed with the timeless sound of a high-quality piano, which is regarded worldwide as a very euphonic instrument, the combination of the two instruments forms a bridge between the two cultures.

The leitmotif of the brand music consists of a pentatonic four-note sequence, striking a balance between Asian and Western cultures. Since the photography style of DKSH has been defined as "natural, honest, personal, sincere, with no effects" it was decided to let the sound follow that route as well: All DKSH music features real instruments and forgoes any type of synthesized sound. As defined in the audio branding workshop, DKSH's tone is intense, passionate, and driving – yet sensitive.

A very special audio element is the natural sound of flowing water weaving its way subtly throughout the DKSH brand sound. In Asia, this sound traditionally carries meaning and significance: Water is one of the earth's four elements, responsible for life and growth. Every religious system on the Asian continent attributes positive imagery and symbolism to water. The sound of flowing water is also a reference to the fantree symbol in the DKSH logo. The fantree is said to be the traveler's companion and water supplier: When a leaf or stem is cut off, water drips out. The fantree has been the symbol of DKSH for over a hundred years.

Figure 4. The fantree symbol in the DKSH

The brand voice was chosen to be male, American, friendly, warm, professional and positive. The brand audit revealed that most voice recordings for DKSH were over-enthusiastic, overly friendly and seen as outright marketing. As a market leader, DKSH has no need to act in such an aggressive, exaggerated way. The new tone of the voice is close, trusted, warm, personable and sensitive.

5. DKSH Audio Applications

The animated sound logo finishes off all DKSH audio-visual materials, such as image films, TV ads and trailers for trade fairs and events. The fantree symbol in the logo appears with a light, watery swoosh and is then followed by the four letters D K S H accompanied by the four notes of the DKSH leitmotif.

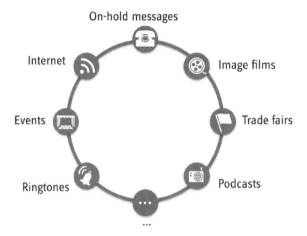

Figure 5. DKSH Audio Touchpoints

A company's phone music is its calling card in the most literal sense of the term, and is often the first point of contact for a business partner – all the more reason to communicate the mood of the brand through this medium. The DKSH brand music is carefully mixed with the brand voice, informing callers in a relaxing and pleasant way.

Especially at high-profile presentations at trade fairs and events, a presentation jingle introducing a speaker creates an impressive and high-quality acoustic framework. The jingle is also based on the DKSH leitmotif. In this application, it is more dynamic than in the brand music, without pushing it over the top.

DKSH ringtones highlight the DKSH leitmotif and support employee identification with the company and its values.

For environments such as reception areas, work places or at events where calm background music is needed, the soundscape is used. This is a background sound installation featuring single notes from the hammered dulcimer, a few guitar bits from the brand music, and the subtle sound of flowing water.

6. Results

The DKSH brand sound has been in use since the end of 2011. The first steps of implementation were marked by numerous international, customized on-hold messages and the integration of the brand music in the official DKSH image film.

A set of audio branding guidelines can be downloaded by employees and agencies from the DKSH extranet.

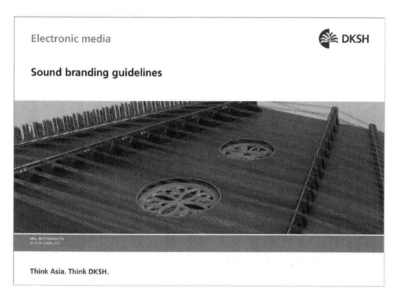

Figure 6. The audio branding guidelines are available as an interactive PDF file.

The DKSH sound has added a strong asset to the brand's corporate identity. It helps transport the brand's tone, adding emotion while strengthening employee identification. It reinforces the brand's recognition and sets it apart from its competitors.

Renfe Audio Branding

Juan Corrales

Flyabit.es

1. The Sound of the Train

Since we were kids, trains have had plenty of room in our personal soundscape archive. Just think of the train sounding as a toy, in movies of the Far West, Far East or hundreds of other films were it has appeared.

Nevertheless there is not an easy audio path to transmit the complex universe of the train. Traditional beloved sounds linked to the train machine in everyone's mind now reflect non ecological and old fashioned values and are likely to be avoided since they don't exist anymore and have little to do i.e. with today's ultramodern magnetic-flying trains. Likewise, the train's personality is vast: the wonderful Orient Express has little to do with a day to day London train to Kingston departing from the Waterloo Station or with the Spanish High Speed train, i.e.

Furthermore, the train, rather than just a transportation vehicle, is a cultural element that many times represents key social, political and economic peaks of the countries. The arrival of the train to the far West was a symbol of the conquering and expansion of the US Nation in the North American Continent just like the Chinese Himalayan train has other political and economic meanings.

As far as Spain is concerned, the train is a central element in the structure and development of the nation and traditionally of utmost importance in connecting all Spanish regions, so diverse and sometimes not easy to connect as far as physical transportations are concerned.

Therefore, the train in Spain has run parallel to the country's development. In the last decades, just like the country entered the EU and grew economically, some important advances happened in the train; High Speed Train (the AVE) arrived in 1992 with the Sevilla Expo and modern applications of the train to today's urban lifestyle came in the form of a big development of the Short Distance-Urban Train (Cercanías). Likewise, the internationalization of the economy, drives the Train industry to reach global spots, such as the huge contract for the Mecca train or other projects to come in the US or Russia.

In terms of branding, the Train in Spain is Renfe and Renfe is the Train. It has been the unique national train operator for decades and is deeply linked to the idea of the train in people's minds.

So what if your brand means "train" to a whole country and has some 99% of awareness, but some huge branding challenges to face? How should your brand sound? This was the case of Renfe.

2. The Challenge

In 2006 Renfe was the only train operator in Spain, recently separated from its infrastucture division (stations and railway tracks) and with a new visual identity after decades of the older one. Nevertheless, branding was tough. Sub brands of the products cannibalized with each other and with the mother brand. Renfe Brand itself had the risk of losing relevance, awareness and meaning. Its values were shifting to other brands.

Four main product divisions existed:

- High Speed (AVE): A very strong brand with big awareness that was taking from the mother Renfe brand values such as innovation, modernicity or technology.

- Long Distance – Regional (Alaris-Alvia): Linked to the traditional territory of the train, with strong values of safety or comfort.

- Freight train: The weakest brand but the strongest business unit, something that had to be leveraged.

- City Train (Cercanías): Close to younger target and modern urban lifestyle, with an important growth, was also taking its share of the brand's values.

Branding order and coherence had to be introduced. A new branding stategy and branding elements should be created so that the mother brand should support and work for product brands and product brands should contribute themselves to build the new mother brand.

3. The Strategic Approach

In an unprecedented move in the Spanish market we bet on the power of sound and music to reach the goals the brand needed. Sound and music proved to be a unique and winning communication tool to succeed on objectives as delicate and diverse as:

- Brand Awareness: The shift in the brand had to be noticeable, something difficult with its strong branding heritage.
- Brand Coherence within all products, sub brands and branding efforts.
- Brand Culture: Everyone in the organization had to look in the same direction: Renfe.
- Introduction and leveraging of values.
- New tools capable to communicate from an emotional and rational/functional way.
- A long term purpose was only possible with a short term success in terms of qualitative and quantitative welcome.
- Feasible implementation: A must. Very possibly the most difficult goal to achieve in such a complex public organization with limited audio branding experience and multiple decition makers.

The Strategic Pillars

Music rather than audio elements had a big weight in Renfe's advertising but had always being used in a piece by piece basis rather than with a real branding thinking. We had to start fron scratch which meant a great opportunity but a challenge extraordinarily difficult to achieve.

Two main sound branding strategic elements were designed:

- A Brand Territory to which every audio output should belong.

- A Sonic Identity that everyone could recognise that must work as the strongest common branding element of most communications.

Music vs Sound Design

It was decided that the sound idea must be based on musical elements with no lyrics rather than sound design.

Many reasons supported the idea:

- Brand DNA: Renfe is a major traditional brand meaning a lot in the "Spain" brand. When communicating, sound in Spain tends to mean, music. Also, Renfe's communications always used relevant music and we wanted to take advantage of it.

- Awareness: easier to produce momentum with music.

- Catchy: We wanted people to remember and be able to reproduce and sing it to others.

- Values: Many brand values had to be communicated. To give all brand information in a single audio piece was impossible. Instead we designed a scheme of multiple pieces of audio sharing the same Renfe Territory. The sum of them all would give the full message, thus avoiding saturation and ear fatigue. Pieces had to be inspired in the same composition but be different. Music, of course, suited better than i.e., a sonic effect. Still the audio logo had to be used in a more consistent way, using advertising pressure to increase awareness.

- No borders: Spain is a complex market and everyone is either a client or target for Renfe. Music (with no lyrics) avoided borders as important as cultural, geographical, age or racial ones, transforming a potential disadvantage into a strength.

- Derivations/Covers: We needed to create a full universe of sound pieces belonging to the same territory/idea. Musical compositions made it possible.

The strategy decided on was to create a central sound solution idea for the main mother Renfe brand and develop it in two ways:

1. Attending to the products / sub brands with their specific sonic territory and musical derivations.
2. Attending to the Touchpoints or channels where sound would be used thus creating specific sound solutions.

4. Down to the Tactics

Sound Logo

The Renfe brand needed to express itself in different ways, from different brands to different targets and moments. As far as the sound logo is concerned, these meant it should always talk with different voices even though a single one (the Marimba voice) had to be the one where the bigger part of efforts would be put to maximize branding goals for the mother Renfe Brand. Therefore, the Sound Logo created is more a musical motif rather than a certain sound. The motif is always the same but it can have different timbre, tempo or mood depending of what is needed either in the touchpoint or in the message.

Music

A central composition had to be created and from it all derivations for products/sub brands and touchpoints came. Once the path to follow was clear, we had to start translating it all to audio. The first main element created was the:

Expressive Sound Territory

An Expressive Sound Territory was defined to guide sound and music creation. It initially permitted few exceptions and was intended to become more flexible in time, allowing new sound ideas to complement the central territory, once it become solid enough. From this Expressive Sound Territory, musical compositions were created for each and every sub-brand, taking into account their specific personality and brand values to leverage. The production also reflected it, from the instruments and arrangements used to the sound productions itself.

Renfe's Expressive Sound Territory Facts

- Mode: Major | Tempo: Mid or slow | Expression: Smooth, slightly melancholic but positive.

- Articulation: Smooth, legato rather than staccato | Tessitura: Sweet and bright.

- Arrangements: Not complicated harmonies | Production: Not too modern textures.

- Pitch: Mid highs, mid lows, highs and lows. | Music vs sound approach: Emotional vs sensitive.

- Example of instruments: Piano, Guitar (smooth attack), Wooden Instruments.

- Analog better than Electronic: Still, all are permitted.

5. The Touchpoints

When defining the main touchpoints, the approach was pragmatic. It was important to produce a feasable and easy plan that shouldn't appear overwhelming. Each touchpoint and the use of the audio pieces produced had to be easy to understand and implement.

In an extaordinarily complex organization with touchpoints managed by very different departments (from communication to product, presidency or customer service) this was a key element. We will depict two touchpoints for their relevance:

Advertising

Music and sound solutions for advertising were produced. Many different covers of the Renfe music were created. For six years, the only music used in TV, radio or any other advertising piece was the Renfe Sound Brand, creating a solid coherence and big awareness.

Train

By far, the most important touchpoint since it is the product itself and the main brand experience for users. A specific sound was designed to be played everytime a train stops or a public announcement message is produced. The sound is the Sound Logo with a Marimba sound. Years before the iPhone, the Marimba seemed an excellent instrument since its sound is both percussive and warm as well as accurate for producing melodies. Furthermore, the technical challenge of the awful sound speakers the trains generally have made it neccessary to produce a simple single voice sound with no harmonies and always within the frequencies these devices emit.

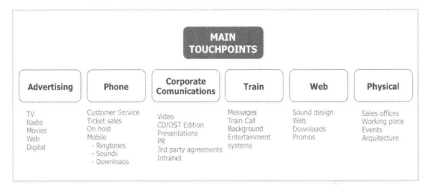

Figure 1. Main touchpoints

6. The Implementation

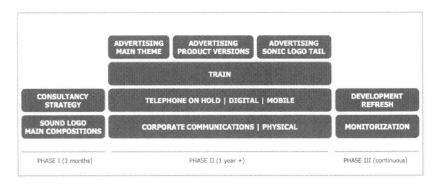

Figure 2. The implementation process

Two key elements were produced to grant an excellent implementation:

1. A Brand Audio Guide: A very simple document including every piece of audio produced and where and how it should be used.

2. The Audio Brand Guardian, belonging to the Renfe Brand office and from where the whole project was implemented.

6. The Results

Results have been overwhelming through the years, addressing every initial goal that was set both on a quantitative and qualitative basis, and very specifically, Audio Branding has proved to be a central key tool in branding strategy.

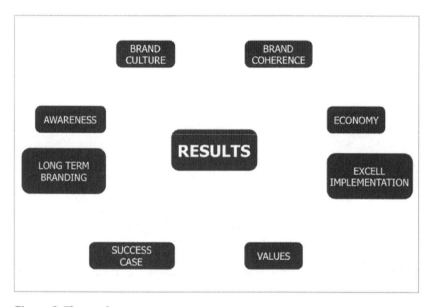

Figure 3. The results

Harrods Case Study

Lydia Watson, Julian Treasure

The Sound Agency Ltd

What happens when one of the world's most famous retail brands meets one of the world's leading audio branding consultancies? The creation of an extraordinary multi-sensory experience, of course!

1. Executive Summary

Harrods is the largest department store in Europe with over one million square feet of retail space, 330 departments and 32 restaurants. It employs 5,000 staff from over 50 different countries and is sited on almost two hectares of land. On peak days it can welcome up to 300,000 customers; most days it receives over 100,000.

Since its purchase by Qatar Holdings in May 2010, the store has embarked on a substantial refurbishment program which will involve the upgrading of the entire store over the coming years. Harrods is currently undertaking a period of expert design consultation involving specialists such as The Sound Agency to create a unique and extraordinary store experience which will continue to attract and delight its customers.

2. Harrods: The Background

Harrods recognized that it needed to improve both the quality and the content of its store sound. Even before the audit by The Sound Agency, it was clear that sound within the store was not designed, was inconsistent, unmanaged, of variable quality and often produced a negative effect on both customers and staff.

Harrods contacted The Sound Agency to see how we could harness the full power of sound and make it congruent with both the Harrods brand values and those of the brands sold within the store. This was both a hugely exciting and innovative challenge for The Sound Agency: to translate this concept into such a large store which is home to thousands of different brands and to reach a huge demographic of customers in a world of retail that never stays still.

3. The Sound Agency: Research and Findings

The Sound Agency carried out a full sound audit of the store using two teams over a period of five days. The audit resulted in the taking of 264 separate measurements, each with a recording and analysis, and resulted in 199 recommendations for action. This was followed by a Brand-Sound™ workshop for the store's sale and marketing team which resulted in 28 tactical recommendations.

The Sound Agency generated a BrandSound™ plan which defined 140 zones within Harrods, proposing 34 playlists and 23 generative sound-scapes. This bespoke plan is unique to Harrods and was created entirely to match their sound requirements. It is designed to deliver a congruent multi-sensory experience for customers throughout the store.

The BrandSound™ plan is truly flexible because it factors in regular refreshing of the playlists and soundscapes so that the sounds remain organic, fresh and are able to reflect ongoing external influences, such as special events, seasonal changes, etc. The systems are future-proofed by the use of state of the art equipment such as the Ambifier™ devices used to play the generative soundscapes.

We believe that this is the first time that such soundscapes have been used in a retail space and we are extremely proud that Harrods are leading the way. Aesthetics naturally play a crucial role in the refurbishment process so The Sound Agency has been very careful to ensure that all sound equipment is aesthetically pleasing. Our collaborative working approach means that all Harrods retail team members can share their opinions on the sound in their department with us at any time.

4. Harrods Toy Kingdom

The new Harrods Toy Kingdom is a paradise for young and old alike. The refurbishment of this department resulted in the creation of five distinct zones, each with its own very clear identity and sound: Big Top, Enchanted Forest, Wonderland, Odyssey and Reading Room. The refurbished Toy Kingdom opened in July 2012 to critical acclaim and to the delight of the tens of thousands of children who have visited since its opening.

Having fully audited this area and discussed the refurbishment plans in considerable detail with Harrods, The Sound Agency were able to create five distinct, appropriate and delightful generative soundscapes which then perfectly matched the area in which they were to be played. A further six special effects sounds were created to add to the magical effect.

The Enchanted Forest zone is a bewitching mixture of real wooden trees amongst which customers can hear forest birdsong containing the sounds of cuckoos, buzzing bees and wind whistling through branches. Smaller children delight at the sound of fairies whispering to them from flower pots at ground level.

In the Big Top zone children are plunged into the world of the circus to the accompaniment of animal sounds from trumpeting elephants, whinnying horses, yapping dogs and monkeys and barking seals. Drum rolls are followed by the sounds of oooohs and aaaahs, laughter, gasps and claps from the audience whilst the Ringmaster extols the crowd to "Roll up! Roll up for The Greatest Show On Earth!"

Speakers placed at variable heights and in the physical fixtures themselves mean that sounds are truly sensational and surround customers as they move around each space and transition from one zone to another.

5. Outcomes and Future Plans

The Sound Agency's work in The Toy Kingdom is a first for the retail landscape in terms of scope and creativity. The success of the launch of the new Toy Kingdom, both externally via overwhelmingly positive media coverage and internally from endorsement at CEO level, has meant that The Sound Agency has been confirmed as the sole provider of strategic sound to Harrods. We have already rolled-out beautiful and custom-designed playlists to the International Designer Rooms for women and to the Children's Wear department and we are now embarking on an even more ambitious plan to produce world-class sound for the rest of the store.

The Sound Agency's work has made a tangible difference to the world of sound in retail environments and has made a significant contribution to the field of audio branding in a truly unique and remarkable way. Our program of enlightening as many members of Harrods staff to the positive power of designed sound that is congruent with the brand is beneficial in two ways; firstly by educating them on the possibilities which exist and secondly by increasing awareness of our work in this industry. Harrods continues to be delighted with the consolidation of their brand identity and the adaptable, future-proof tools we have used to provide their sound.

The Sound Agency is truly thrilled to have had such an impact in a prestigious store such as Harrods. We have successfully demonstrated the potential for well-designed sound in the retail environment as an alternative to generic music. In combination with the incredible work that Harrods has undertaken in terms of the refurbishment itself, we have contributed to the establishment of an extraordinary multi-sensory experience which ensures that Harrods remains one of the world's truly unique retail destinations in its own right.

Show Me The Metrics! Validating Effectiveness of Dell's Audio Identity System™ Assets

Rayan Parikh, Susan Aminoff

Elias Arts LLC

1. Executive Summary

Over the past three years, Dell Inc. has embarked upon one of the most ambitious and comprehensive audio branding programs of any Fortune 500 company. Essential to this effort was the need to demonstrate meaningful and attributable return on investment for Dell's audio branding program. This article details how Dell and its audio branding partner, Elias Arts, developed an audio branding program that:

- bolsters Dell's long-term business and branding goals
- includes key assets quantifiably measurable in effectiveness
- shows how audio assets are "moving the meter" on Dell's brand performance

The research demonstrates that the tested audio assets significantly improved the perception of the Dell brand as well as increased the efficacy of tested advertising among target audiences in key global markets. Further analysis also provided key insights into which tested audio assets could propel Dell's long-term strategic branding, marketing and communications needs forward. Taken as a whole, the research program is a compelling case for the viability and importance of branded audio.

2. Elias Arts and Audio Branding Research

Brand-based audio assets are transitioning from "nice-to-haves" to "must-haves" in corporate marketing and communications toolkits. With this transition comes the requisite expectation that brand-based music and sound assets be measured against the same types of performance metrics as any other advertising or marketing tool.

With over three decades' experience developing brand-based music and sound for businesses, Elias Arts has conducted and overseen a diverse array of audio performance metrics and validation programs for global brands. Elias has applied multiple audio testing tools and methodologies (e.g. focus groups, surveys, usability testing, in-field observation, neurometrics, ethnographic research, etc.) to many brands, including Orange, IBM, Verizon Wireless, American Express, and Harrah's Casinos. For all clients, Elias Arts' overarching philosophy is that defining the goals of an audio branding research program is subject to the same criteria as any broader audio identity program: business objectives first need to be clarified and defined, and then a determination of how the audio identity system can help realize those objectives needs to be established.

3. Dell – Brand Background

Beginning in early 2010, Dell embarked on a company-wide initiative to redefine the company's mission and establish an aspirational (and quantitatively-based) positioning and personality for the brand. At the time, the company's enduring reputation as the "USD399 pink laptop" brand was inconsistent and out of step with its growing leadership position in the global enterprise IT market. Over the course of several months of in-depth research and analysis, the Dell brand team developed a strategic brand platform that defined the aspirational brand personality and "voice" of the brand.

In addition to clarifying Dell's long-term business objectives, the brand personality data provided Elias Arts with key insights into the optimal strategic approach to developing and executing a holistic Audio

Identity System™ (AIS) to align with Dell's aspirational goals for both business and brand. In-depth interviews with diverse stakeholders, as well as vetting brand attribute-linked music concepts/needledrops, helped Elias formulate how different instrument combinations and musical elements correlated with – and best expressed – desired existing and aspirational brand attributes. Aggregating these "right-brain/left-brain" data points was a critical foundational input in all of Elias' audio branding work for Dell.

As the core foundational components of Dell's Audio Identity System™, two final treatments of audio logos (short-form brand music) and audio thematics (long-form brand music) were selected for field testing and validation. The fielded studies were designed to answer key overarching questions:

- How does the emotional registration of each audio asset align with Dell's aspirational brand personality and existing brand research?

- What perceptual differences (if any) exist across country markets, cultures and/or target audiences?

- Which audio treatments best enhance Dell's brand engagement in the marketplace going forward?

As the brand's "sonic positioning statement", Dell's brand thematic was designed to ensure the music would align with Dell's brand personality and design attributes. Given that all assets in Dell's audio identity system would emanate from – and be inspired by – the thematic, it was critical the foundational efficacy of the thematic treatments be ascertained and validated first through research.

3.1 Dell Thematic – Research Design and Insights

In order to generate rich, open-ended feedback from focus group participants on the instrumental and emotional elements of the thematics, a qualitative survey protocol was designed in partnership with Elias and Dell's independent research partner to comparatively evaluate the two final thematics ("T2" and "T4") across key global markets. Testing was conducted with groups listening to both tracks (no brand association) and then having each participant build collages by selecting words and images that represented their feelings associated with each track. The tracks were then qualitatively evaluated in the broader context of the brand set (Dell plus competitors), and then vis-a-vis Dell specifically.

After testing the thematics across markets and audiences, some clear insights began to emerge. Both themes were perceived as accessible, culturally appropriate, and effective at creating a richer, more defined personality for Dell (which was perceived up to that point as having limited differentiating brand characteristics). The key difference between the two musical assets lies in how each theme emphasized different components of the Dell brand personality. Whereas thematic T2 appropriately reflected the positive perceptions of Dell today, thematic T4 did a better job of projecting and reinforcing a future image of Dell. This data provided some clear feedback to determine which thematic aligned more closely with Dell's brand goals, one that is forward-looking, conveys momentum, dynamism and empowerment.

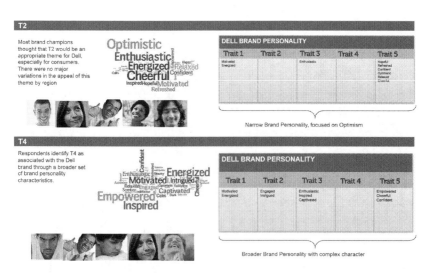

Figure 1. Brand Personality Analysis – Thematic T2 vs. T4

3.2 Dell Audio Logo – Research Design and Insights

Since the audio logo design work was coordinated with the thematics, the research could advance further by testing the logo vis-a-vis the visual Dell brand as well as within marketing touchpoints which would leverage the selected audio logo. A 15-minute online survey was crafted and administered to a total of 1200 participants representing a cross-section of Dell's target audiences. The respondents were comprised of 600 enterprise-level IT Decision Makers (ITDMs) and 600 Consumers (various sub-profiles) across three markets (US, UK and China).

Sample groups evaluated the two final audio logos ("V3" and "V5") in the same context. Each audio logo treatment was slated on top of the visual Dell logo at the end of a single TV advert. Respondents were exposed to each ad version then exposed to each audio logo version in isolation. Additionally, original versions of the adverts without audio logos were exposed to the groups. Building off these exposures, a variety of questions were asked to assess the audio logos in relation to brand impact and communications effectiveness.

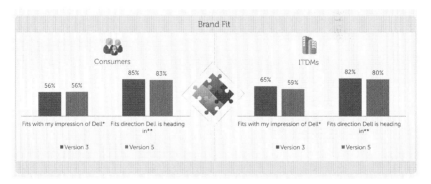

Figure 2. Audio Logos Comparative Brand Fit – Consumers vs. ITDMs

Across all three markets, both logos demonstrated a strong fit with existing perceptions of the Dell brand. Additionally, when respondents were asked to evaluate if the logos "fit the direction Dell is heading in", both audio logos performed well. This was a strong indication that both logos could not only align with (and enhance) current marketing and communications, but also have a proactive effect on building Dell's aspirational brand personality.

Respondents were also asked to cite the first few words, thoughts or feelings that immediately occurred to them after they heard each audio logo. Using word cloud analysis, perceptual distinctions between the "personalities" of each audio logo became clear.

Figure 3. Word Clouds – Audio Logo V3 vs. V5

The word clouds illustrate that audio logo-V3 elicited spontaneous associations with Happy, Catchy and Upbeat. Audio logo-V5, despite producing a less defined response, moved the needle on areas such as Power and Strength, which are more closely aligned and associated with Dell's strategic communications pillars and aspirational goals.

Additionally, both audio logos had a positive and salient affect when coupled with the sampled advertising. 82% of respondents globally noticed the audio logos in sampled advertising when prompted (unsurprisingly, unaided recognition was relatively low, given that respondents had never heard the audio logo prior to the research). Moreover, a significant percentage of respondents in all markets strongly agreed both audio logos made the sampled ad more appealing based on a variety of diagnostic statements. The top 2 boxes ("Completely Agree" and "Agree") scored comparatively high for both Consumers and ITDMs (average of 35% and 53% respectively).

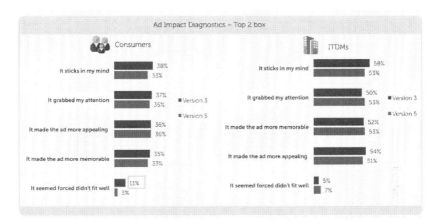

Figure 4. Audio Logos in Sampled Advertising – Consumers vs. ITDMs

Delving further, the research indicated that ITDMs felt a greater affinity for both audio logos compared to the Consumer group. That is, both logos shifted perceptions and increased favorability of Dell more significantly across the board for this key constituency:

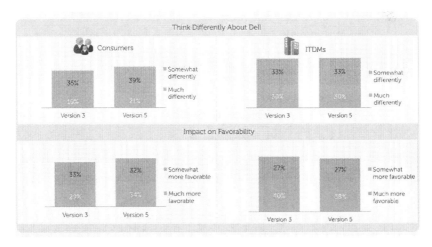

Figure 5. Audio Logo Comparative Favorability – Consumers and ITDMs

111

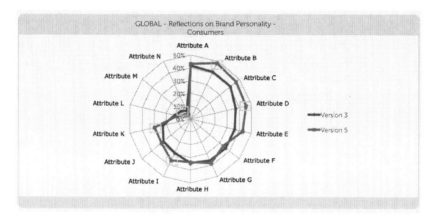

Figure 6. Brand Personality Assessment, Consumer Group – Audio Logo V3 vs. V5

Audio logo V5's alignment with personality characteristics preferred by IDTMs made it the final recommendation because it aligned with growing market segments for Dell in the corporate enterprise space and enabled Dell to strengthen its brand reputation and brand permissions in this area. Furthermore, audio logo V5 scored well with Consumers and thus would not alienate what continues to be a significant revenue base for the company. In short, audio logo V3 represented how the Dell brand is perceived today, whereas audio logo V5 better personifies how the Dell brand aspires to be perceived going forward.

4. Best Practices

While Dell is only one of many clients with whom Elias Arts has undertaken audio research, this study demonstrates several best practices that typically recur regardless of clients' research protocols and/or objectives:

Research inputs really do affect music design outputs: While music certainly isn't something that benefits from being quantitatively "boxed in" or broken down into generic elements, the Dell study did provide the desired metrics and insights to show a strong connection between the process-based inputs Elias uses to design the music and the high performance marks the assets received in research and testing. Hence, these inputs can make the art and craft of music even more powerful than it would be otherwise.

Start with the business objectives, and work backwards to design the right research program: Often research programs are designed to answer a lot of questions that do not ultimately address the desired objective. Investing time and effort in clarifying what the audio assets need to accomplish on behalf of the business objectives – and how they should help meet those objectives – will inevitably lead to research programs both efficient in scope and revealing in nature.

Track success metrics over time, as well as signs of wear-out and/or listener dissonance: All people form different relationships with pieces of music over time; a popular mnemonic can become tomorrow's annoying cliché. It is therefore critical to continue assessing brand music over time, not only for what it is positively contributing to the brand, but also for its potential liability to the brand over time.

Consider context: Researching and evaluating audio assets in and of themselves are important to understanding how the assets connect back to the brand conceptually. It is no substitute, however, for understanding how music and sound are experienced within a given context. Whether it is an advert, a physical space or a device, sounds have to be assessed as part of the greater environment in which they are experienced.

Facilitate partner agencies' use of/need for audio branding assets: In most cases, other client agencies (advertising, events, PR, digital, etc.) are key collaborators to activating brand-based audio assets. Not only will these partner agencies need assurance that audio branding assets can advance their client/campaign objectives, these agencies are also obligated to demonstrate ROI in all components of their marketing spends. Therefore, whenever possible, incorporate research that helps agencies make the case for inclusion of audio branding assets in their work.

Show Me The Metrics!

Elias Arts' research and validation program with Dell demonstrates that while music is, and will continue to be, the *"universal language of emotion,"* this famous reference by Tolstoy does not preclude audio brand assets from also being quantifiably measured and evaluated on an objective basis. The noteworthy success and efficacy of both tested logos in this case further demonstrates that audio plays a critical role in increasing brand value, and can demonstrably accelerate the improvement of key brand performance metrics of all types.

The Linde Group: The Story Behind a Unique Audible Identity

Michele Arnese, Rudi Mauser

amp – audible brand and corporate communication

1. Audio Branding in the Context of The Linde Group

The Linde Group is one of the world's leading suppliers of industrial, process and speciality gases, and one of the world's most profitable engineering companies. Linde products and services can be found in nearly every industry, and in more than 100 countries.

Why is The Linde Group searching for a sound identity of its own? What connects a technology and engineering company with the emotions of music?

Linde stands for over 130 years of technological progress. Technology, innovation and an inventive spirit have characterised the company from the very beginning. Carl von Linde's curiosity as an inventor, his persistence in the implementation of his ideas and theoretical concepts, as well as his ability to recognise the requirements of his customers and fulfil their desire for reliability and quality are all timeless factors for success.

Along with his curiosity and persistence, he had a deep love of music, intended as the highest expression of art and shared in the family circle with passion and discipline. The Linde family – throughout the generations – used to make music at a very high amateur level, playing classics and performing "house concerts".

Hence the decision for The Linde Group to start developing its own sound identity has its roots in the history of the company, together with several major goals that we describe in the following text.

1.1 Emotionalise the company's transformational journey

Linde has been on a transformational journey to reshape the company for several of the past years. In March 2006 Linde made a proposal to acquire The BOC Group, Linde's major competitor. The acquisition was completed on 5 September 2006. Following the acquisition, the combined gas and engineering group was rebranded as The Linde Group, and the materials handling activities were separated and rebranded as well. In 2005, Linde AG and BOC together had 21% of the world's market in industrial gases, so following the BOC acquisition, The Linde Group became the world's largest industrial gas company.

The first goal of Linde's audio branding was to emotionalise in music the message of becoming one company, one culture, one brand, in order to foster a feeling of belonging to one great team.

As the CEO writes in a personal message to employees:

"Music forms an integral element of culture – it brings its spirit to life. Our common culture is what binds us together, through the values we live and the inner conviction we share. We have translated this spirit into music, into the Linde Suite. It is a musical journey through time, from the early days when our company was founded, all the way to its most recent transformation and our rise to a truly global player. Our very own music shall now accompany us on our journey to become the High Performance Organisation we are striving to be. It shall give us a feeling for the pleasure of creating our very own unique profile."

1.2 Increase brand uniqueness

One of the reasons The Linde Group decided to start developing audio branding was to improve brand uniqueness with the key element of a sound identity. With a better integration of all aspects of the brand personality, The Linde Group achieves a better association with its mission and products.

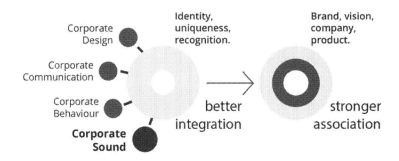

Figure 1. Role of corporate sound

The goal of adding an audible dimension to the newly developed brand identity was necessary in order to build a strong common identity among all the brands in the group and to emotionalise the brand experience. Furthermore Linde's products, gases, are invisible and inaudible, so giving The Linde Group a sound identity also means bringing the products closer to the people.

1.3 Add an emotional dimension to an engineering focused, technical communication

Audio branding at The Linde Group is also a way to add an emotional dimension to the company's communication, which is very technical and focused on engineering. The communication takes advantage of this new emotional dimension, especially if it makes use of techniques such as storytelling – music helps to transmit the message and secure it in the memory.

2. The Development of Audio Branding at The Linde Group

After doing a brand audit and developing a strategy to meet the goals and needs of Linde's sound identity, we described the strategy in a paper that also contained the creative briefing for the DNA of Linde's sound identity: the brand theme and the brand sound.

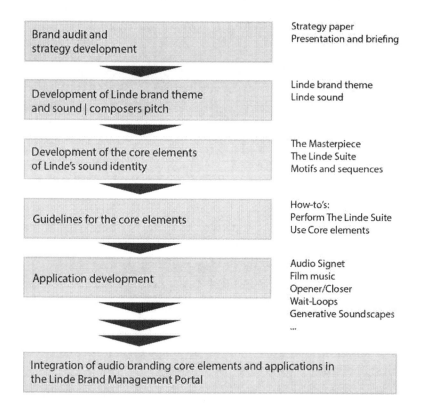

Figure 2. Audio branding development process

We started the creative development with a composer pitch and finally with an assessment to find out which deliverable has shown the best way to 1) represent the brand and 2) be flexible, memorable and recognisable. The brand compliance was proven by matching the music with brand communication language and brand visual language.

The core elements of Linde's sound identity, The Masterpiece and The Linde Suite, together with motifs and sequences, are the basis for the further development of a wide range of applications that enable the brand to be heard in different situations. Based on the core elements, we continued and focused the development of a set of applications to make the brand audible at different touch-points and in different situations.

2.1 The Linde brand theme

The nucleus of Linde's brand theme is a 4-tone motif:

Figure 3. The Linde brand theme

We gave the melody a small range – two minor thirds in a row, with a fourth as the biggest interval – and kept it relatively short.

The benefits are:

singable	Everybody can sing this melody very easily...
memorable	and if somebody can sing a melody very easily, they will also memorise it quickly.
flexible	And this melody is very flexible, making it easy to include in a new arrangement or composition –in whatever musical style. The 4-tone nucleus "E-G-F-D" is taken from the pentatonic scale. Every culture – in Asia, Africa and the Western world – uses a pentatonic scale. Not only does every culture have a pentatonic scale, this scale also provides the basis for many modern musical styles, like jazz and pop music.

If we focus on the "brand compliance" between the Linde brand theme and the Linde brand, we can identify some key properties of the Linde brand theme and their equivalents in the brand communication of The Linde Group:

a.   *The Linde brand communication is focused...*

In the first part we have a repeating sequence of the same tones (an interval of a third) – in contrast to a playful melody, for example,

b.   *...but not introverted.*

The melody takes an unexpected turn on a suspended note, in other words: the second part of the melody creates tension. Or you could also call this the expressive part of the melody.

c.   *The Linde brand communication is drawn from life ...*

The minor third interval in the first part is very familiar to everybody: When we want to get somebody's attention, we often sing out: Hello!

d.   *... but not simplistic.*

We don't resolve the melody into the tonic, but surprisingly into the dominant in a so-called half cadence.

2.2 The Linde sound

The Linde sound is a real orchestral sound. Here too we have kept the brand in mind, and especially the translation of Linde's visual branding language into sound:

	Linde's visual language	The Linde sound
Authenticity	Natural, not sterile or glossy depictions	Real orchestral sound
Clarity	Subtle and homogenous colour spectrum	
Generosity	Different perspectives and sections	

Considering the claim of The Linde Group – and its equivalent in internal communication – there is also a perfect fit with the Linde sound:

	Linde claim	Linde sound
External communication	LeadIng	Lead voice (brand theme) is taken from different orchestra sections
Internal communication	I am taking the lead	

2.3 The structure of the core elements of Linde's audio branding

Beginning with the Linde brand theme, we started developing different core elements of Linde's audio branding in order to build a pool of new branded music. The Masterpiece is the first piece, composed in the style of a contemporary score and produced with a real symphony orchestra.

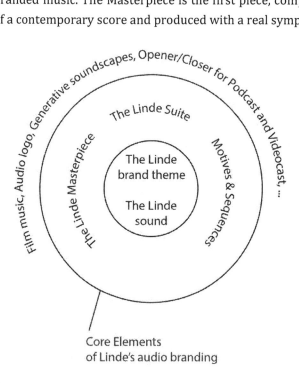

Figure 4. Structure and hierarchy of Linde's audio branding

After the Masterpiece we realised The Linde Suite, an orchestral suite in four movements, that describes in 30 minutes the 130-year-long history of the company. Together with the Masterpiece and The Linde Suite, we have a bundle of motifs and sequences that we use in different pieces of music, complementary to the Linde brand theme, in order to gain a good balance between creative flexibility and brand sensibility.

2.4 The Linde Suite

The music is played by a classical symphony orchestra, supplemented by ethnic and electronic instruments. This takes you on an awe-inspiring journey through four epochs and the most important phases of the company's history – every movement has been realised in the musical style of the corresponding epoch and takes the versatile Linde brand theme on this musical journey.

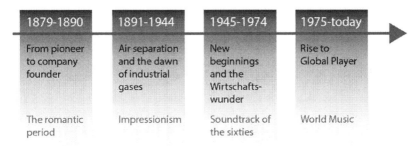

Figure 5. Concept behind The Linde Suite

The music joins tradition with the future, like the brand does, reflects the company's values, can be used all over the world and can be performed by a wide variety of different ensembles. The Linde Suite was set up by amp as an international project: Los Angeles, Vancouver, Cologne, Munich and Bratislava were stations in the realisation of a musical work where the composer, orchestration, arranger, orchestra and the agency contributed to an amazing result. The Suite is used as the basis for the production of other components of the audio branding and as an emotional and effective piece of music for staging events all over the world (corporate events, brand merger events, award ceremonies, etc.) to make the Linde spirit a memorable and lasting experience. An experience that all Linde employees worldwide are intended to share. After the successful premiere at the Linde Management Conference in 2010, the Linde Suite was sent as a CD to all employees around the globe – as audible evidence of a common identity and accompanied by a personal greeting from the CEO (see paragraph 1.1).

2.5 The Linde sound identity has been built on the core elements

Using the core elements, or parts of them, integrating them with new concepts and musical ideas, we realised many applications of Linde's sound identity that enable the brand to be heard and to establish an audible way to communicate in different situations, touch-points and media. Here are some examples:

Film Music	We created film music for different videos, films and trailers, for the Internet / Intranet and for events.
Audio Signet	Taking the Linde brand theme, we created an audio signet to be used in various media. We combined the brand theme with a sound generated by shooting compressed air onto a specially tuned harp that resonates the brand theme harmony. The aim of using a combination of music and sound was to create a "*contextualised*" audio signet, with a direct association to the products of The Linde Group: the air.
Generative Soundscapes	Using musical fragments from the Linde brand music and of course, from the core elements of Linde's sound identity, and combining these with sounds from different categories (industrial / gas, nature and environment, urban life, etc.) we realised generative soundscapes that can be configured to be used in different situations.

3. Spreading the Message

Brand music is used in different forms for all media in internal and external communication. The branding and communication team at Linde and the event and design agencies working for Linde are now aware of the advantages of having a tool that delivers the right audio support for all communication activities. Since 2010, the Linde communication team has been using The Linde Suite for several major brand change events worldwide. A strong brand ambassador, a story-teller and an entertainment element in one. For the 2012 Management Conference in Shanghai, we realised the Linde Suite Part II: the journey continues. A new symphony celebrating the determination to be number one in the world and a great demonstration of the continuity in the emotional approach based on sound identity for internal communication at Linde. The best measurable result of the development process for a B2B company like The Linde Group is the fact that requests for using the brand music often came directly from local communication teams: the best way to prove that music finds its own way.

4. Outlook

A sound identity has to be continually developed, enhanced, extended – so the process at The Linde Group is still evolving, even after 3 years. One operative step we are working on is to integrate all the elements of Linde's sound identity, all applications and guidelines into the Linde Brand Management Portal in order to give all communication, marketing and branding employees worldwide direct access to the sound material. One conceptual step we are working on consists in the "contextualisation" of Linde brand music in two subcategories, healthcare and clean technology, in order to create branded music that can be used in the corresponding divisions, unifying the branding aspects with The Linde Group and its special businesses, each of which requires a different musical expression.

For a selection of audio contributions related to the Case Study "The Linde Group", please visit:

http://audio-branding-academy.org/aba/congress/audio-branding-award-2012/case-submissions/linde-group/

Call for Papers 2012

For the Audio Branding Congress 2012, the Audio Branding Academy announced a call for scientific papers. The topics were "Audio Branding", "Consumer Research", and "Multisensory Design/Communication". After a pre-selection by the Audio Branding Academy and the reviews by the members of the Advisory Board, the following papers were accepted as talks respectively as poster presentations.

Talks

Poster Presentations

Product-Related Sounds Speed up Visual Search

Klemens Knöferle, Charles Spence

Department of Experimental Psychology, Oxford University, UK

Key Words

visual search, sound, object localization, crossmodal enhancement, semantic congruence

Abstract

Consumers often search for specific products in cluttered visual environments, such as the supermarket aisle. The question we address here is whether cues from other sensory modalities might be used to facilitate, guide, and/or bias visual search toward a particular brand or product (type). Prior research suggests that characteristic sounds can facilitate visual object localization (Iordanescu et al., 2008, 2010). Extending these findings to an applied setting, we investigated whether product-related sounds would facilitate visual search for products from different categories when arranged in a virtual supermarket shelf.

The participants identified a target product significantly faster when the visual target was accompanied by a congruent rather than by an incongruent sound. These results extend the facilitatory crossmodal effect of characteristic sounds on visual search performance described earlier to the more realistic context of a virtual shelf display, thus showing that characteristic sounds can speed the rate at which actual products are localized.

1. Background

Searching for the product you want can be a challenging business. It has been suggested that the typical shopper may see as many as 1,000 different products and brands per minute while strolling down the aisle of their local supermarket (Robinson, 1999). From a marketing perspective, the question therefore arises as to whether cues from a shopper's other senses can be used to facilitate, guide, and/or otherwise bias their visual search toward a particular brand, product, or product type. The idea here is not altogether new inasmuch as there has already been some discussion of the use of aroma (fragrance) to direct people's visual attention to items of a particular colour (see Demattè, Zampini, Spence, & Pavani, 2009).

Recently, for example, researchers have demonstrated that the presentation of a particular scent can be used to improve the speeded detection of target objects that happen to be congruent with the scent, even in complex visual scenes (Seigneuric, Durand, Jiang, Baudouin, & Schaal, 2010; Seo, Roidl, Müller, & Negoias, 2010). Here, we address the question of whether product-related sounds can also be used to direct a person's visual search to a particular object/product within a display. If this were to be the case, it might well have profound implications for the multisensory design of retail environments and promotional activities. Specifically, the potential crossmodal effects of auditory in-store advertisements and auditory cues in TV advertisements and digital marketing campaigns would likely have to be reconsidered.

In general, the detection of objects may be visually facilitated by at least two different audio-visual mechanisms. On the one hand, a spatially congruent sound may facilitate visual detection by locally enhancing visual processing in the region of the sound source (such spatial interactions likely rely on crossmodal links in spatial attention; see Spence & Driver, 2004). On the other hand, an object-congruent sound (e.g., a snake hiss) may facilitate visual detection by enhancing the global processing of target-congruent features (e.g., a snake-like, elongated shape; this would be an example of an object-specific interaction;

Iordanescu et al., 2008, 2010). The present research was designed to examine the latter mechanism in a marketing context.

2. Experiment

A single-target visual search task (Quinlan, 2003; Treisman & Gelade, 1980; Wolfe, 1992) was used in order to study the effect of product-related sound on visual processing. Both the experimental design and the procedure closely resembled those used by Iordanescu et al. (2008). However, instead of presenting objects from different categories (e.g., coins, dogs, trains) with exceptionally unique and well-established object-sound relationships, the current research included products that are commonly available in the setting of a supermarket. In each trial, four product pictures were presented in a 2 × 2 search display (see **Figure 1**). The product pictures were randomly chosen from a set of nine possible product pictures, with one product being the target and the remaining three products constituting the visual distractors. On each trial, the auditory stimulus was either consistent with the target (target consistent), consistent with one of the distractors (distractor consistent), consistent with one of the products not presented in the trial (unrelated), or absent (control condition).

2.1 Participants

Thirty-five undergraduate students and faculty members at Oxford University gave their informed consent to participate in the study (21 female, mean age = 27 years). The participants were compensated with £5 for their participation. All of the participants reported normal or corrected-to-normal vision and normal hearing.

2.2 Stimuli

Each visual search display showed a virtual store shelf containing four different products, one of which was the target, while the remaining three served as distractors (see **Figure 1**). The four products were randomly selected from a total set of nine branded products belonging to different categories (e.g., food, beverages, personal hygiene), and can typically be found in a supermarket: Sparkling wine, potato crisps, bacon, whipped cream, deodorant, bath gel, facial tissues, and a digital camera. The visual stimuli were shown on a 17 inch CRT-monitor; each picture was scaled to fit within a 10.5° by 9.1° area. For each product, we sourced a typical sound either of the product itself (e.g., camera shutter sound), of its packaging (e.g., champagne bottle opening sound), or of a related event (e.g., a sneezing sound for the facial tissues). The duration of the sounds varied between 250 and 2500 msec due to the distinct nature of the recorded events. The sounds were played back via two loudspeakers positioned one on either side of the screen at an average sound level of 70 dB and did not carry any spatial information.

Figure 1. Example of visual search display

2.3 Procedure

The participants were seated in a darkened, sound-proof experimental booth approximately 60 cm from the screen. The experiment was self-paced, with participants starting each trial by pressing the space bar. The name of the target product (e.g., "Walker's crisps") appeared on-screen for 1000 msec, followed by a fixation cross in the centre of the screen. After 350 msec, the participants were presented with the visual search display containing the target and three distractor products. The visual display was randomly accompanied by a target-congruent sound, a target-incongruent sound, an unrelated sound, (with the auditory cue preceding the visual stimulus by 100 msec), or else no sound. Congruent sounds were semantically related to the target (e.g., uncorking a champagne bottle), incongruent sounds were related to the product shown in the opposite corner of the display, and unrelated sounds did not correspond to any of the products shown in the display. Participants indicated, as rapidly and accurately as possible, the location of the target product by pressing "f", "j", "v", or "n" for the upper left, upper right, lower left, or lower right screen quadrant, respectively. Each trial ended with a 500 msec feedback screen indicating whether or not the participant had responded correctly or not. Participants were given a practice session consisting of 12 randomly selected trials (three from each condition). Then, they completed six blocks, each consisting of 36 trials, that is, nine trials for each of the four experimental conditions. It should be noted that the participants were instructed not to pay special attention to the sounds, but to fully focus their attention on the search task.

2.4 Results

One participant whose average reaction time (RT) was more than two standard deviations above the average RT of all participants was removed from further analyses, as were trials with RTs lower than 100 msec (.76%) or greater than 2000 msec (.43%). An additional .29% of the trials were removed due to measurement error (unusually high onset delays in the RT measures, probably due to unscheduled CPU load during measurement).

A repeated-measures analysis of variance (ANOVA) revealed a statistically significant difference in target localization latencies across different sound conditions, $F(3, 99) = 2.99$, $p < .05$, $\eta^2_{partial} = .083$. Post-hoc tests using the Bonferroni correction confirmed that participants found the target product significantly more rapidly when the sound was congruent ($M = 578$ msec, $SD = 133$ msec) rather than incongruent ($M = 595$ msec, $SD = 138$ msec) with the target ($p < .05$). All other pairwise comparisons were non-significant. There was no significant difference in response accuracy as a function of the experimental condition, $F(3, 99) = 1.160$, $n.s.$, and no obvious speed-accuracy trade-off. The findings are summarized in **Figure 2**.

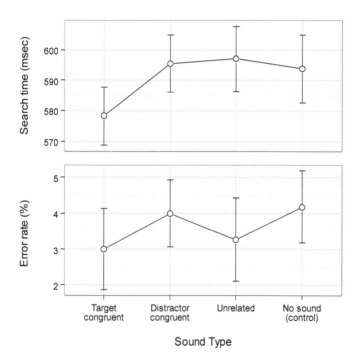

Figure 2. Visual target search RT and error rate as a function of different sound conditions (target congruent, distractor congruent, unrelated, no sound). Error bars indicate the 95% within-subjects confidence intervals (Morey, 2008).

3. Discussion

The present results extend the facilitatory crossmodal effect of characteristic sounds on visual search performance reported recently (Iordanescu et al., 2008, 2010) to the more realistic context of a virtual shelf display. While in Iordanescu et al.'s research, the links between auditory and visual stimuli can be regarded as well-learned and easily accessible (e.g., the image of a cat and a meowing sound) and the stimuli were drawn from vastly different categories (animals, instruments, everyday objects, etc.), the present study used auditory-visual stimulus pairs that featured more ambiguous relationships and that were drawn from a single category (i.e., supermarket products). To summarize, the results suggest that characteristic sounds can crossmodally enhance the visual processing of objects in realistic, everyday situations such as while strolling down the aisle of a supermarket. In practical terms, playing characteristic product sounds in retail environments may help shoppers to more rapidly detect the products associated with these sounds among other, distracting products.

The pattern of results reported here rules out a non-specific facilitatory effect of auditory stimulation. In general, auditory stimuli are known to have a general alerting effect that temporarily increases phasic alertness in participants (Petersen & Posner, 2012), thus resulting in reduced search latencies. However, such a general alertness-related effect would typically be associated with a speed-accuracy trade-off that is not consistent with the present results. In addition, the fact that distractor-congruent and unrelated sounds did not significantly impact search latencies indicates that the facilitation by target-congruent sounds cannot solely be attributed to increased attentional arousal induced by the presence of some form of auditory stimulation.

In addition to implications for retailing, the present research also bears relevance for online marketing. In many instances, web pages can be regarded as visual search tasks, with different stimuli competing against each other for the limited attention of the user. If product-related sounds are indeed able to improve visual search performance for a specific element on a web page (such as a product in an online shop or a banner advertisement), they may be used to guide the user's attention to this specific element.

In the light of the present results, future research could study the effects of congruent versus incongruent sounds using even more realistic and cluttered visual displays (e.g., with 9, 16, or more products) that more fully reflect the complexity of real-life shopping environments (see, e.g., Garber, Hyatt, & Boya, 2008). Finally, given that not all consumer products have a typical sound that is linked to their use or consumption, researchers could test whether verbal auditory cues (i.e., spoken product names) have a similar facilitatory effect on people's visual search performance. Following up on this question may also help to inform earlier research reporting improved visual recognition performance for objects when they were preceded by their associated sounds, but not when preceded by their spoken names (Chen & Spence, 2011).

References

Chen, Y.-C., & Spence, C. (2011). Crossmodal semantic priming by naturalistic sounds and spoken words enhances visual sensitivity. *Journal of Experimental Psychology: Human Perception and Performance, 37*(5), 1554-1568.

Demattè, M. L., Zampini, M., Spence, C., & Pavani, F. (2009). Do odour-colour associations bias the orienting of visual attention? *Chemical Senses, 34*(3), 42.

Garber, L., Hyatt, E., & Boya, Ü. (2008). The mediating effects of the appearance of nondurable consumer goods and their packaging on consumer behavior. In H. N. J. Schifferstein & P. Hekkert (Eds.), *Product experience* (pp. 581-602). London: Elsevier.

Iordanescu, L., Grabowecky, M., Franconeri, S., Theeuwes, J., & Suzuki, S. (2010). Characteristic sounds make you look at target objects more quickly. *Attention, Perception, & Psychophysics, 72*(7), 1736-1741.

Iordanescu, L., Guzman-Martinez, E., Grabowecky, M., & Suzuki, S. (2008). Characteristic sounds facilitate visual search. *Psychonomic Bulletin & Review, 15*(3), 548-554.

Morey, R. D. (2008). Confidence intervals from normalized data: a correction to Cousineau (2005). *Tutorial in Quantitative Methods for Psychology, 4*(2), 61-64.

Petersen, S. E., & Posner, M. I. (2012). The attention system of the human brain: 20 years after. *Annual Review of Neuroscience, 35*, 73-89.

Quinlan, P. T. (2003). Visual feature integration theory: past, present, and future. *Psychological Bulletin, 129*(5), 643-673.

Robinson, J. (1999). *The manipulators: a conspiracy to make us buy*. London: Pocket Books.

Seigneuric, A., Durand, K., Jiang, T., Baudouin, J. Y., & Schaal, B. (2010). The nose tells it to the eyes: crossmodal associations between olfaction and vision. *Perception, 39*(11), 1541-1554.

Seo, H.-S., Roidl, E., Müller, F., & Negoias, S. (2010). Odors enhance visual attention to congruent objects. *Appetite, 54*(3), 544-549.

Spence, C., & Driver, J. (Eds.). (2004). *Crossmodal space and crossmodal attention*. Oxford, UK: Oxford University Press.

Treisman, A. M., & Gelade, G. (1980). A feature-integration theory of attention. *Cognitive Psychology, 12*(1), 97-136.

Wolfe, J. M. (1992). The parallel guidance of visual attention. *Current Directions in Psychological Science, 1*(4), 124-128.

Implicit and Explicit Effects of Music on Brand Perception in TV Ads

Daniel Müllensiefen[1,2], Christopher Davies[2], Lauri Dossman[2], Jon Ludvig Hansen[1], Alan Pickering[2]

1 Department of Psychology, Goldsmiths, University of London
2 DDB UK

Key Words

music in advertising, advertising pre-testing, implicit association test, semantic differential

Abstract

The paper describes a novel empirical method for matching music to consumer brands based on Asmus' (1985) semantic differential for music. In Exp. 1 the method is applied to thelselection of congruent and incongruent music for four TV ads for a juice brand. Exp. 2 measures the effect of the two types of music as well as silence on the persuasiveness of the ads by an effectiveness index derived from an advertising pre-testing questionnaire as well as by change in implicit attitudes towards the brand measured by reaction time in an Implicit Association Test (IAT). Congruent music significantly enhanced the effectiveness of at least one tested ad and in addition, the IAT test showed significantly positive attitudes towards the brand. However, no significant changes in implicit attitudes were found due to the influence of the music.

1. Introduction

Pre-testing advertisements is standard in modern marketing but there has been little research directly assessing the effectiveness of the various sensory components of an advert, including any music used. This paper addresses this lack of research. In the first part of the paper we describe the development of a new tool based on Asmus' Semantic Differential (1985) for assessing the fit of individual music pieces to the profile of a given brand and how this tool can be used to select music that maximises brand fit. In the second part we evaluate the effects of music, that is congruent or incongruent with the brand profile, on the perception of different TV commercials for the same brand. As evaluation techniques we use an industry-standard questionnaire asking explicitly for participants' judgements, as well as an adaptation of the Implicit Association Test (Greenwald, McGhee, & Schwartz, 1998) to assess implicit attitudes towards the brand. Hence, part two of this paper evaluates whether the 'best-fit' music identified in part one actually enhances brand perception, and explores whether the effects of music can be seen both implicitly and explicitly.

1.1 Music in advertising

Music is widely used in adverts (Stewart & Koslow, 1989; Applebaum & Haliburton, 1993) and the trade journal Admap claimed in 2003 that music can help to gain attention, create desired moods, change the pace of an advertising narrative, and facilitates brand and message recall. Academic research since Simpkins and Smith (1974) has confirmed this belief (see review in North & Hargreaves, 2008), and has elicited various theoretical accounts (e.g. Gorn, 1982; MacInnis & Park, 1991).

1.2 Assessing the fit between music and brands

MacInnis & Park (1991) suggested that music aids the processing and perception of ads when the 'fit' between product/brand and music is high: i.e. if music matches the message of an ad (cf. non-message-matched music) it will have predictable effects on the processing of an advert. Hung (2001) suggests that congruent music might reduce semantic noise and set a stronger focus on the cultural context and communicative meaning of the ad. The notion of musical fit thus appears to enhance the message of an advert, fostering positive purchase intentions and attitudes towards the product advertised.

While the theoretical notion of musical fit has an intuitive appeal and is supported by a good amount of empirical evidence (e.g. Hung, 2001; Zander, Apaolaza-Ibañez, & Hartmann, 2010), the general problem of measuring the fit between a piece of music and a brand has not been satisfactorily resolved. The solution we suggest here is based on the assumption that the main mechanism that connects music with advertised brands or products is affective processing. We therefore used an established instrument for the measurement of the affective content of music and adapted it to assess the emotional profile of a commercial brand. Distance and closeness ("fit") between an arbitrary number of music tracks and a brand can then be measured by standard methods using the same dimensional space.

Asmus (1985) devised a multi-dimensional measurement tool for assessment of musical affect, based on the semantic differential (SD) technique developed by Osgood, Succi, and Tannenbaum (1957). The SD involves rating a given stimulus over a wide range of different attributes. In an experimental session, individuals rate the extent to which they consider each term to be an appropriate description of a particular stimulus. Asmus (1985) compiled a selection of adjectives deemed appropriate for describing a wide range of affective responses for music. After repeated factor analysis, he identified 3 individual factors.

The 3 broad factors were termed 'vibrancy', 'morose' and 'serenity'. Each of these dimensions was divided into 3 sub-dimensions. Several studies have reported successful use of this 9-dimension measurement tool (Coffman et al., 1995; Miller & Strongman, 2002). In experiment 1 we use Asmus' semantic differential to measure the multi-dimensional profile of a range of musical pieces as well as profile of a widely-known juice brand and subsequently identify the pieces with a minimal distance (i.e. optimal fit) to the brand.

2. Experiment 1

2.1 Method

The aim of this experiment was to determine the effectiveness of a semantic differential technique based on a pre-determined factor structure in terms of its ability to differentiate between different musical soundtracks. This effectiveness is gauged in two different ways: A) Whether or not songs that were originally determined to be congruent with the brand profile of a chosen fast-moving-consumer-goods (FMCG) brand were *more* congruent than possible alternatives, or indeed congruent at all and b) whether or not the semantic differential technique works equally well with individuals of differing levels of musical sophistication and across genders.

Four TV ads for the chosen orange juice brand from the last 10 years were selected. Each had been at the centre of a large advertising campaign and had been broadcast on UK television for at least several weeks. Each ad had an original music soundtrack of about 40 seconds that was clearly audible and with the exception of a spoken sentence in the last five seconds that was identical in all four ads. The soundtrack did not contain any speech. Each campaign used a very different theme/narrative but all campaigns were created to convey the same image of the juice brand that had been unchanged over the last 10 years.

For the derivation of the brand profile six members of staff from DDB UK, who had been working as account managers or account planners for the juice brand for several years, scored the brand on the 7-point rating scale of the 39 adjective items of the semantic differential.

For each ad, three alternative tracks were selected to match the original soundtrack in style, genre, instrumentation and, if possible, performing artist, with regard to its affective content. The alternative tracks were chosen according to the 3-factor structure of semantic differential (one track for each of the three dimensions), giving a bank of sixteen songs altogether. Selection of the alternative tracks was based on the musical expertise of three of the authors, but each track was unanimously agreed upon. From each, a 40s excerpt was extracted to match the length of the original soundtrack.

Participants were recruited mainly online, and covered a wide range of nationalities. Altogether there were 185 respondents (96 females, 89 males). Their ages ranged from 18 to 84 years (M = 30.15, SD = 12.13). Most participants rated four randomly selected songs on the semantic differential (although a small number of participants gave between one and three responses). On each of the four trials, the participants' task was to listen to the music clip and to imagine that the music would portray a film character. Then, they were instructed to rate the film character on the 39 adjectives of the semantic differential. The fit of each song to the juice brand was then calculated in terms of the Euclidean distance of each song from the brand profile. These Euclidean distance measurements were based on each song's scores on each of the 3 factors and the distances of these scores from the consensus brand image scores generated by the advertising professionals.

2.2 Results

The juice brand loaded heavily on the vibrancy factor, but also the serenity factor (average scores of 51.25 and 48.75 respectively). The overall score on the morose factor was, as expected, comparatively low 15.25). Ratings from online participants were averaged across all 16 songs. Euclidean distances across the 3 dimensions were then calculated between the profile of each individual song and the juice brand profile. The original soundtracks as well as the alternative tracks loading high on vibrancy were always significantly closer to the brand profile than the songs loading high on the morose and serenity dimensions (all p's < .05).

For assessing the general suitability of the semantic differential for a wide audience we performed k-means cluster analysis and divided the participants into two groups according to their musicality level. Paired samples t-tests showed no significant difference between the ratings of either group on any of the three dimensions according to musicality, nor were there any significant differences between the two genders.

2.3 Discussion

As indicated by the results, the semantic differential method was able to differentiate between songs in terms of their distance from a desired brand profile. In addition, the participants' judgements on the semantic differential indicated that the original songs, as well as the songs assumed to load high on the vibrancy factor associated with the juice brand, had clearly the lowest distance from the brand profile. This confirms our initial hypothesis and indicates the face validity of the semantic differential as a research tool. In sum, this technique allows advertisers to determine where a particular soundtrack lies in a three-dimensional semantic space relative to a desired brand image. This helps advertising practitioners to match music and brand as closely as possible, so as to ensure congruency during an advertisement. The semantic differential used here also seems widely applicable in that there were no significant differences between individuals of different levels of musicality and gender.

3. Experiment 2

While experiment 1 demonstrated the usefulness of the semantic differential to distinguish and select music pieces with respect to a target brand, the purpose of experiment 2 is to investigate whether a small distance between brand and musical pieces does indeed help the effectiveness of a TV advert in terms of attitude changes.

By far the most common way of (pre-)testing ad effectiveness is to use standardised questionnaire instruments where question items index features of the advert such as persuasion, brand/product awareness (Brown, 1986), engagement, enjoyment etc. Usually, data norms for ads from the same product category are available for comparison and are used to interpret the effectiveness of an ad in absolute terms. For the purpose of this experiment we are using a generic questionnaire that was modelled on several questionnaire instruments currently in use by market research companies. We will refer to this method as the 'explicit testing procedure' as participants are asked explicitly about their perception of the ad.

However, there seem to be limits to the applicability of explicit questionnaire instruments (Feldwick, Carter, & Cook, 1991), especially in situations where people are either not aware of their own attitudes or are incapable of assigning verbal statements for explaining their behaviour or where judgements are assumed to be distorted by subjective beliefs and biased introspection (Nisbett and Wilson, 1977). However, many tests have been developed to reveal preferences and attitudes without relying upon explicit and conscious judgement formation (Schacter, 1989). As an alternative to the generic explicit pre-testing questionnaire, we chose to employ an adaptation of the Implicit Association Test (IAT; Greenwald, McGhee, & Schwartz, 1998) to assess ad effectiveness with an implicit measurement technique. The IAT works on the basis that "if two concepts are highly associated, the IAT's sorting tasks will be easier when the two associated concepts share the same response, than when they require different responses" (Greenwald & Nosek, 2001 p. 85). The IAT is a reaction time (RT) task. In one of the initial experiments reported by Greenwald et al. (1998) expected combinations of terms (flower names + pleasant words) yielded significantly shorter RTs than less expected combinations (insect names + pleasant words). The same test framework has also been effective in measuring implicit preferences towards consumer brands (Maison, Greenwald, & Bruin, 2004). For this study, we adapted the IAT paradigm to also measure ad effectiveness as attitude change towards a brand as a result of watching a TV ad. Hence, in contrast to previous applications of the IAT in advertising research (e.g. Hari & Forestier, 2012), our participants had to take the IAT twice, before and after watching an ad. We hypothesised that reaction times would decrease when responding to target-concept words (i.e. words associated with the brand) after seeing an advert with congruent music (i.e. music with a low distance from the brand profile). Conversely, we expected reaction times (RTs) to remain unchanged or even increase if participants were exposed to an ad with incongruent music or no music at all. In accordance with the standard IAT methodology, we used a water brand for comparison to the target juice brand in order to control for practice effects. If reactions for the target juice brand are significantly reduced compared to reactions for the water brand this would indicate the effectiveness of an associative priming effect generated by the combination of music and ad.

3.1 Method

The experiment used the same four TVs ads that formed the basis for experiment 1. According to the results of experiment 1, we selected the four tracks that matched most closely the juice brand profile as well as the tracks that were judged as most distant from brand profile. In addition, all four TV ads were also presented without any music (but retaining the spoken message at the end of each spot). Crossing the four TV ads with the three music types created twelve different conditions on which we tested 259 participants (most frequent age bands 18-25 years (n=101) and 26-34 years (n=88); 43.6% women) in a between-subjects design. The explicit questionnaire, as well as the IAT, were implemented as an online test together with the actual ad using the Qualtrics multimedia testing framework.

Participants were first acquainted with the IAT procedure by running two practice trials. After that participants completed three consecutive runs of the IAT before watching a TV advert, paired with congruent, incongruent or no music depending on the participant's condition. This was followed by another three runs of the IAT. RTs from the three runs before and after watching the ad were compared to assess the effect of the ad condition implicitly. As the last component of the experimental procedure participants responded to the explicit questionnaire asking participants' about their perception of the ad.

3.2 Results

Explicit questionnaire
In accordance with industry standards we combined five rating scale items from the explicit questionnaire to index the effectiveness of the ad. One item measured the enjoyment of the ad, three items indexed engagement with the ad and one item reflected how well the brand was

linked to the message of the ad. Ratings from all items were z-transformed and the three engagement items were averaged before adding them to the other two items. The resulting effectiveness score ranged on a scale from about -7 to 8 and was normally distributed.

We analysed the effectiveness score with a linear mixed-effects model with music condition (congruent, incongruent, no music) as fixed effect and ad campaign (4 different campaigns) as random effect. According to the model there was a significant effect of music condition $(F(2,244)=3.79, p = .024)$. Bonferroni-corrected pair-wise comparisons between all three conditions revealed that there was a significant difference $(p= .024)$ between congruent music and no music but not between incongruent music and either of the two other conditions as shown in **Figure 2**.

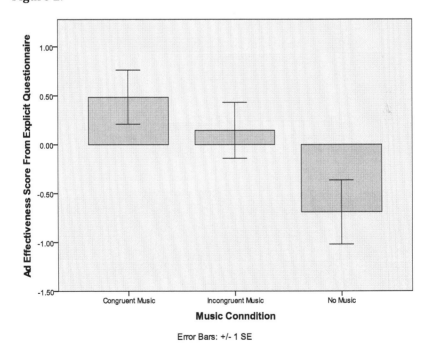

Error Bars: +/- 1 SE

Figure 2: Means of the ad effectiveness score for the three music conditions. Error bars indicate +/- 1 standard error.

In order to determine whether the effect of music interacted differently with the four different ad campaigns we ran a model-based partitioning analysis (Strobl et al., 2009) which indicated that the music conditions impacted differently on participants' explicit ratings for ad campaign 3 compared to the other three campaigns. For campaign 3, congruent music does indeed differ significantly from incongruent as well as from no music as hypothesised (p< .05) while for the other 3 campaigns differences between congruent and incongruent music are smaller and not significant.

Implicit brand attitudes

With regards to the implicit attitudes towards the juice brand and changes of these attitudes, we looked for two different effects in the RT data from the IAT task. Firstly, we hypothesised that participants would generally have positive attitudes towards the brand and therefore reaction times prior to seeing the ad should be shorter for brand attributes being paired with positive attributes as when paired with negative attributes. Secondly, any positive influence of watching the ad should manifest itself in shorter reaction times for brand attributes paired with positive attributes after seeing the ad compared with the same condition before the ad. Because the sorting of positive/negative attributes together with the brands relied on the speed with which participants responded with their right/left hand we included self-assessed handedness of the participant as a predictor variable.

We ran a mixed-effects model on with positive/negative attribute pairing and handedness as fixed effects and participant and item as random effect using only the log-transformed reaction times from the two pre-ad trials for the juice brand. Attribute pairing ($t(2969)=2.864$, $p=.004$) as well as the interaction between attribute pairing and handedness ($t(2969)=-2.473$, $p=.013$) proved to be significant predictors in the model while handedness as a main effect did not reach significance ($t(2969)=0.544$, $p=.586$). As hypothesised reactions for the trial where the brand attributes were paired with negative attributes were generally slower and this effect even was significantly stronger for the left-handed participants as can be seen from the means in **Table 1**.

	Attribute Pairing	Handedness	Mean Reaction Times (SD) in miliseconds
1	positive attributes	left	917 (377)
2	negative attributes	left	1035 (508)
3	positive attributes	right	936 (366)
4	negative attributes	right	948 (394)

Table 1. Means and standard deviations of (untransformed) reaction times to juice brand attributes when paired with positive as opposed to negative general adjectives.

To identify any change in the implicit attitudes towards the brand due to watching the ad we ran a mixed-effects model with a full factorial design using music condition, attribute pairing, pre-post ad viewing and hand-edness as fixed effect predictor variables and participant, item, and ad campaign as random effects. We hypothesised that a 4-way interaction effect between these variables would indicate the effect of the music condition. However, the 4-way interactions did not reach significance level, neither for the contrasts between congruent and incongruent music nor for congruent music vs silence (p > .5 in both cases). In fact, none of the 24 main and interaction effects in this model reached significance.

4. Discussion

In this paper we have described a principled and empirically grounded way for matching music pieces to consumer brands and quantifying the distance between a brand and a piece of music. This novel research tool enables advertisers and market researchers to identify music that either fully reinforces the emotional values of a brand or deliberately associates a brand with emotional labels that it is less associated with. The tool is simple, easy to score and it is equally suitable for participants regardless of their gender or musical background.

In the explicit evaluation of the effectiveness of TV ads (with congru-ent or incongruent music or silence) via a post-experiment questionnaire we found significantly higher effectiveness scores for congruent music than silence as well as significantly higher scores for congruent vs. in-congruent music, but only for one out of the four ads tested. The finding that the difference in effectiveness scores between congruent and incon-gruent music was not significant for the other three ads might be ex-plained by the fact that both types of music tracks were matched on a number of important attributes, such as artist, genre, musical era etc. Thus while the emotional content of the tracks differed, there might have still been a musical fit between brand and music that was created by the attributes the tracks had in common (see Zander et al., 2010). Thus, in a follow-up experiment it would be interesting to see whether consumers' interpretations of TV ads can differ due to different musical soundtracks while the effectiveness of the ads remains unchanged. If this hypothesis was true then it would be appropriate to speak of several possible 'musi-cal fits', at least for certain types of ads.

Similar to IAT applications in previous advertising research we were able to measure significant implicit attitudes towards the target brand. However, we were not successful in measuring any change in implicit at-titudes comparing the results from the runs of the IAT before and after watching the ad. There are several potential reasons for this failure to observe a change in attitudes. First it is widely accepted that implicit atti-tudes in general, and consumer attitudes in particular, change slowly (see review by Gawronski & Bodenhausen, 2006). Thus, it is possible that several viewings of the same ad might have been required in order to observe significant changes in implicit attitude. A second possibility is the time consuming nature of our experimental setup may have weak-ened the effects via fatigue, order effects and large individual differences. In addition, data collection was carried out over the internet reducing our ability to control the conditions under which the experiment was taken. Finally, the argument that the same ad can have a good fit with dif-ferent kinds of music might also apply to the absent effects for implicit attitudes.

Thus, we conclude that the initial results from using the semantic differential as a tool for selecting music to enhance the effectiveness of TV ads are encouraging and warrant further research. Future research would need to focus on the characteristics of certain ads that interact with the impact of different types of music. In addition, whether change in implicit attitudes is observable using the IAT is unresolved and warrants further research.

Acknowledgements

We are grateful for the support with this project from Sarah Carter and Les Binet from DDB UK as well as Orlando Wood from BrainJuicer. We also like to thank Katharina Bauer who helped with the preparation of the manuscript.

References

Appelbaum, U., & Halliburton, C. (1993). How to Develop International Advertising Campaigns that Work. International Journal of Advertising, 12 (3), 223-241.

Asmus, E. P. (1985). The development of a multidimensional instrument for the measurement of affective responses to music. Psychology of Music, 13(1), 19-30.

Brown, G. (1986). Modelling Advertising Awareness. Journal of the Royal Statistical Society. Series D (The Statistician), 35(2), 289-299.

Coffman, D., Gfeller, K., & Eckert, M. (1995). Effect of textual setting, training and gender on emotional response to verbal and musical information. Psychomusicology, 14, 117-136.

Feldwick, P., Carter, S., & Cook, L. (1991). How Valuable is the Awareness Index. Market Research Society 1991 Conference Papers, 137-150.

Gawronski, Bertram, & Bodenhausen, Galen V. (2006). Associative and propositional processes in evaluation: An integrative review of implicit and explicit attitude change. Psychological Bulletin, 132(5), 692-731.

Gorn, G. J. (1982). The effects of music in advertising on choice behavior: a classical conditioning approach. Journal of Marketing, 46(1), 94-101.

Greenwald, A. G., McGhee, D. E., & Schwartz, J. L. K. (1998). Measuring Individual Differences in Implicit Cognition: The Implicit Association Test. Journal of Personality and Social Psychology, 74(6), 1464-1480.

Greenwald, A. G., & Nosek, B. A. (2001). Health of the Implicit Association Test at Age 3. Zeitschrift für Experimentelle Psychologie, 48 (2), 85-93.

Hari, J., & Forestier, C. (2012). The thin win: Implicit preference for slim models in advertising. Academy of Marketing Conference, Paper 131.

Hung, K. (2001). Framing meaning perceptions with music: The case of teaser ads. Journal of Advertising, 30(3), 39-49.

MacInnis, D. J., Park, C. W. (1991). The differential role of characteristics of music on high- and low-involvement consumers' processing of ads. Journal of Consumer Research, 18(2), 161-173.

Maison, D., Greenwald, A. G., & Bruin, R. H. (2004). Predictive Validity of the Implicit Association Test in Studies of Brands, Consumer Attitudes and Behaviour. Journal of Consumer Psychology, 14(4), 405-415.

Miller, M., & Strongman, K. (2002). The emotional effects of music on religious experience: A study of the Pentecostal-charismatic style of music and worship. Psychology of Music, 30(1), 8-27.

Nisbett, R., & Wilson, T. (1977). Telling more than we can know: Verbal reports on mental processes. Psychological Review, 84, 234-259.

North, A. C., & Hargreaves, D. J. (2008). The social and applied psychology of music. Oxford: Oxford University Press.

Osgood, C. E., Suci, O. J., & Tannenbaum, P. H. (1957). The measurement of meaning. Urbana: University of Illinois Press.

Schacter, D. L. (1989). On the Relation Between Memory and Consciousness: Dissociable Interactions and Conscious Experience. In H. L. Roediger & F. I Craik (Eds.), Varieties of Memory and Consciousness. Essays in honour of Endel Tulving (pp. 355-389). Hillsdale, NJ: Erlbaum.

Simpkins, J. D., & Smith, J. A. (1974). Effects of music on source evaluations. Journal of Broadcasting, 18(3). 361-367.

Stewart, D. W., & Koslow, S. (1989). Executional factors and advertising effectiveness – a replication. Journal of Advertising, 18(3), 21-32.

Strobl, C., Malley, J., & Tutz, G. (2009). An introduction to recursive partitioning: rationale, application, and characteristics of classification and regression trees, bagging, and random forests. Pychology Methods, 14(4), 323-348.

Zander, M., Apaolaza-Ibanez, V., Zander, & Hartmann, P. (2010). Music in advertising: Effects on brand and endorser perception. In Terlutter, R., Diehl, S., & Okazaki, S. (eds). Advances in Advertising Research (Vol. 1). 127-140. Wiesbaden: Gabler Verlag.

Linking Theories of Emotion-Induction to Applications in Audio Branding

Hauke Egermann

Audio Communication Group, Technische Universität Berlin

Key Words

music, emotion, affect, mechanism, application

Abstract

This article presents an overview of recent theoretical and empirical work on emotion, music, and corresponding links to applications in audio branding. Theoretical mechanisms explaining emotional effects of music will be described, including cognitive appraisal, brain stem reflexes, rhythmic entrainment, musical expectation, emotional contagion, visual imagery, conditioning, and episodic memory (Juslin & Västfjäll, 2008, 2010). Furthermore, it will present research testing these mechanisms and aims to illustrate how this scientific knowledge may be applied to audio branding using musical elements as emotion-inducing stimuli.

1. Emotion in Audio Branding

The article will provide a review of theory and research on emotion, music and corresponding links to applications in audio branding. But why should one focus on emotion? Emotions are generally considered as affective and adaptive responses to internal or external events, manifested as simultaneous activity in several components (Scherer, 2005). These are often categorized into four groups: a) cognitive appraisals of those events on several evaluation dimensions; b) subjective feelings that function to monitor the affective state of a person; c) peripheral psychophysiological arousal that in turn prepares d) behavioural responses, that communicate emotional responses via bodily expressions (including voice, face, and/or gesture) and create motivations to certain adaptive behaviours (e.g. approach vs. avoidance, fight vs. flight). Thus, affective responding is important to understand as emotions guide behaviour by creating motivations to approach stimuli that elicit positive emotional responses like happiness and avoid those that elicit negative responses like fear, disgust, or anger.

Accordingly, understanding which events elicit which emotional responses allows predicting human behaviour, a matter that is also considered important in consumer behaviour research (Hirschmann & Holbrook, 1982). Purchase decisions, attitudes towards ads, products, and brands are very likely to be influenced by consumers' emotional reactions to them (Bagozzi, Gopinath & Nyer, 1999). Thus, marketing strategies often target emotional responses through communication measures, including audio branding. Audio branding is generally understood as all consumer oriented acoustical corporate communication activities (Bronner, 2005). These include for example audio logos, jingles, soundscapes, that all often contain musical features like melodies, rhythms, or harmonies. In general, music as part of marketing communication has often been discussed as eliciting various effects on consumers in advertising settings that have been summarized *Attitude Towards the Ad Music* including cognitive and affective components (Lantos & Craton, 2011).

The latter component will be in the focus of this presentation, because comprehensive theoretical accounts to underlying mechanisms have only been presented recently (Juslin & Västfjäll, 2008, 2010). In order to make informed decisions about appropriate music use in marketing contexts, knowledge about those psychological mechanisms that are involved in emotional responding is indispensable. Therefore, this article presents an overview of theoretical positions explaining emotional listener responses to music and their experimental testing. Finally, also possible applications of this knowledge for using music in audio branding will be discussed.

2. Theories and Research About Music-Induced Emotion

A first attempt to summarize corresponding theory and research was presented by Scherer and Zentner (2001), who described several central and peripheral emotion production routes, incorporating appraisal, empathy, memory, and peripheral arousal. In two more recent reviews, Juslin and Västfjäll identified several similar psychological mechanisms (2008, 2010) that are thought to be involved in emotion induction through music: cognitive appraisal, evaluative conditioning, visual imagery, episodic memory, musical expectancy, brain stem reflexes, emotional contagion, and rhythmic entrainment (**Figure 1**).

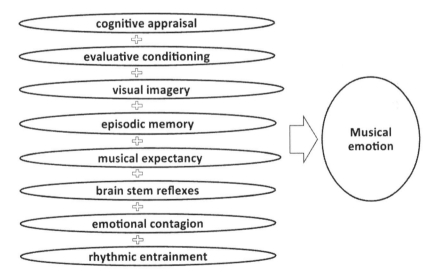

Figure 1. Features and mechanisms involved in auditory emotion induction (Juslin & Västfjäll, 2008, 2010).

Cognitive appraisal is thought to be involved in creating an emotional response to music when the music listened to and the corresponding situation are evaluated. Here emotions are thought to emerge from a cognitive appraisal on several dimensions like novelty, urgency, coping potential, norm compatibility, or goal congruence (see also Scherer, 1999). In an internet-based study, we could show that music emotion ratings are affected by social feedback about the ratings of fellow study participants, interpreted by a social appraisal process where music appraisals were influenced by peer opinions (Egermann et al., 2009).

The next mechanism called *brainstem reflexes* occurs when basic acoustical characteristics (e.g. sudden, dissonant, or loud sounds) of any auditory stimulus signals importance to the human brain. For example, a sudden increase in loudness in the music may provoke a startle response in the listener. Creating sensory dissonance by spectral manipulations of recorded music decreased the pleasantness of induced emotions in western listeners and participants from a native African population that was isolated from western cultural influences (Fritz et al., 2009). Employing a similar research design, we could also demonstrate universal responses to basic music features like loudness in a similarly isolated African population, indicated by higher activations of the peripheral nervous system (Egermann et al., 2012, in preparation).

Rhythmic entrainment occurs when internal body activity synchronizes with external musical rhythms, an effect that could be also observed in the previously cited experiment, in which music with a faster tempo universally increased bodily activations (Egermann et al., 2012, in preparation).

Furthermore, *visual imagery* is thought to induce emotion during listening when emotional mental images are built up by music. However, this mechanism has yet to be studied experimentally.

Music is also thought to affect emotions by violating or confirming listener *expectations*, a mechanism extensively discussed by music theory scholars (Huron, 2006; Meyer, 1956), and that has only been recently studied. Steinbeis et al. (2006) reported that harmonic expectancy violations induced increased emotional intensity and physiological arousal.

Furthermore, we could show that, also in a live concert experiment, violations of melodic expectations were correlated with emotional responding in several response components (subjective feeling and peripheral arousal, Egermann et al., 2011, in press). Furthermore, it was shown in the same study that a computational model allowed predicting the subjective experience of expectation, using machine-learning algorithms to simulate auditory statistical learning.

There are two other mechanisms that are based in memory processes suggested as being involved in musical emotion induction. *Evaluative conditioning* refers to an unconditioned positive or negative stimulus that is paired with the music and affects the emotional response to it. *Episodic memory* is thought to be involved when emotional episodes are memorized together with a specific piece of music. To my best knowledge, both mechanisms have not been experimentally researched.

Emotional contagion describes the internal "mimicking" of emotional expression in the music. Another similar phenomenon is *empathy* that might be attributed to musicians (Scherer & Zentner, 2001). Emotional responses to music might be based on both: a) empathy with a performer or composer to whom expressions might be attributed to (Scherer & Zentner, 2001), and b) a rather automated unconscious contagion through internal mimicking of expressive cues in the music (Juslin & Västfjäll, 2008). However, both phenomena can be understood as very related, because they create emotional responses that match those being expressed. In a first experimental investigation on empathy and emotional contagion, we could show that they moderate, if expressed emotions are felt in the listener (Egermann & McAdams, 2010, in press). Furthermore, music preference ratings strongly influenced empathy.

All mechanisms described are suggested to work in parallel and create emotional responses that might also be of different valence. By listening to only one piece a very rich and mixed emotional experience might be generated. For example, violations of expectation can induce surprise, and additionally sadness that is due to the emotional contagion produced through sad expressions in the piece (slow tempo, minor mode, small melodic ambitus). These emotions can then even be coupled with happiness if a positive event that is associated with the song is remembered (episodic memory).

3. Application of Knowledge About Emotion Induction Mechanisms to Audio Branding

Several theories have been proposed that explain how the use of audio elements and music may affect consumer behaviour: classical conditioning, the Elaboration Likelihood Model (ELM), and musical fit (North & Hargreaves, 2008). All three mechanisms have affective components, as conditioning describes the transfer of effects from unconditioned emotional (e.g. music) to conditioned stimuli (e.g. an advertisement, a product, or brand). According to the ELM, emotional effects of advertising music paired with products and brands will be only effective, if the consumer is in a low involvement state, processing information in a peripheral route of persuasion. However, if the music used fits in its characteristics to those of the product or brand that is being advertised, additional information about the brand can be communicated also in highly involved consumers (Zander, 2006).

These three theories could be partially confirmed by empirical evidence, however, as pointed out by North and Hargreaves (2008), several contradictory results were reported, that were assumed to be caused by a lack of specificity of theoretical models employed and an often rather experimenter-focused definition of music-product fitting. However, one might also assume, that also a deeper understanding of emotional qualities associated with musical stimuli could advance theory and practice on these issues. Thus, considering again the previously explicated mechanisms involved in music emotion induction, several implications for conditioning effects through music can be described.

Mechanism	Emotional Effect	Cultural Impact/ Learning
Cognitive appraisal	All possible emotions	Very high
Brainstem reflexes	Arousal/Sensory pleasantness	Very low
Rhythmic entrainment	Arousal	Low
Musical expectation	Arousal/Surprise/ Pleasure/Tension/ Disappointment	High to medium
Empathy/Emotional contagion	Basic emotions	Low
Visual imagery	All possible emotions	High
Evaluative conditioning	Basic emotions	High
Episodic memory	Basic emotions/ Nostalgia	Very high

Table 1. Emotional effect of and cultural impact on mechanisms (adopted from Juslin & Västfjäll, 2008, 2010).

The different mechanisms create different emotional responses (**Table 1**). Some mechanisms described operate on a rather lower automated level of music processing, some on a rather higher, indicating that effects produced by them are to some degree culturally universal and others highly individual, creating different responses in different listeners. As a consequence, using music with varying degrees of low-level acoustical characteristics (loudness, tempo, sensory dissonance), might lead to low-level universal consumer responses like increased or decreased arousal. However, knowing if a specific target group remembers specific emotional events with a specific piece of music, might also allow predicting emotional responses for that specific consumer subgroup.

Mechanism	Based on Structure	Computational Predictability
Cognitive appraisal	Unknown	Unknown
Brainstem reflexes	Low-level features (loudness, roughness)	High
Rhythmic entrainment	Low-level features (tempo, periodicity)	High
Musical expectation	Complexity/ Information Content	High, identify emotional peaks
Empathy/Emotional contagion	Low- and high level features	High to medium
Visual imagery	Unknown	Unknown
Evaluative conditioning	Indirect	Low
Episodic memory	Indirect	Low

Table 2. Structural link and computational predictability of mechanisms

Other mechanisms are more focused on structural aspects of the music composed or performed that might be computationally analysed in future software systems to predict emotional effects in marketing contexts (**Table 2**). For instance, we could forecast emotional responses to unexpected musical events by means of structural analyses through a computer model (Egermann et al., in press). That way we identified potentially emotional peak moments. Vermeulen et al. (2011) showed for example that synchronous (vs. asynchronous) presentation of brand name and musical peak moment improved attitude towards the ad. Furthermore, already existing software toolboxes can be used to extract sound features that allow to predict which emotional expressions are recognized in a piece of music that might then be internally mimicked by empathy and contagion in a consumer audience. Here, previous research has shown that this is more likely if, in general, the music matches listeners' preferences (Egermann & McAdams, in press). Thus, knowing consumers' music preferences might allow to predict, when for example a sound or piece expressing sadness also induces sadness, and then in turn might be associated with the advertised product through conditioning.

However, as theory and research on music and its emotional effects is still in its very beginnings, all conclusions previously presented must remain speculative. More focused work is needed that expands and specifies the theories and tests derived hypotheses. Regardless, if future efforts are fruitful, I believe that several conclusions can be made from this work, including further recommendations for applications in practical marketing efforts employing music as part of audio branding strategies.

References

Bagozzi, R. P., Gopinath, M., & Nyer, P. U. (1999). The Role of Emotions in Marketing. Journal of the Academy of Marketing Science, 27(2), 184–206.

Bronner, K. (2005). Audio-Branding: Akustische Markenkommunikation als Strategie der Markenführung. München: Grin.

Egermann, H., Fernando, N., Chuen, L., McAdams, S. (2012). Cross-Cultural Emotional and Psychophysiological Responses to Music: Comparing Western Listeners to Congolese Pygmies. Proceedings of the 12th International Conference of Music Perception and Cognition 2012, Thessaloniki, Greece.

Egermann, H., Fernando, N., Chuen, L., McAdams, S. (in preparation). A Cross-Cultural Investigation of Emotional and Psychophysiological Responses to Music: Comparing Western Listeners to Congolese Pygmies.

Egermann, H., Grewe, O., Kopiez, R., & Altenmüller, E. (2009). Social feedback influences musically induced emotions. The Neurosciences and Music III: Disorders and Plasticity: Ann. N.Y. Acad. Sci., 1169, 346-350.

Egermann, H. & McAdams, S. (2010). Recognition is Different From Feeling: Experimental Evidence for Two Different Types of Emotional Processes in Music Using a Between-Subjects Design in a Web Experiment. Proceedings of the 11th International Conference of Music Perception and Cognition, Seattle, WA, USA.

Egermann, H., & McAdams, S. (2011). Expectation and Emotion in a Live Concert Experiment. Psychophysiology. Special Issue: Society for Psychophysiological Research Abstracts for the Fifty-First Annual Meeting Westin Boston Waterfront Hotel, Boston Massachusetts September 14–18, 2011, Volume, 48, S84.

Egermann, H. & McAdams, S. (in press). Empathy and emotional contagion as a link between recognized and felt emotions in music listening. Music Perception.

Egermann, H., Pearce, M., Wiggins, G. & McAdams, S. (in press). Probabilistic models of expectation violation predict psychophysiological emotional responses to live concert music. Cognitive Affective Behavioral Neuroscience.

Fritz, T., Jentschke, S., Gosselin, N., Sammler, D., Peretz, I., Turner, R., Friederici, A. D., & Koelsch, S. (2009). Universal recognition of three basic emotions in music. Current Biology, 19(7), 573-576.

Hirschman, E. C., & Holbrook, M. B. (1982). Hedonic Consumption: Emerging Concepts, Methods and Propositions. Journal of Marketing, 46(3), 92–101.

Huron, D. (2006). Sweet Anticipation: Music and the Psychology of Expectation. Cambridge: MIT Press.

Juslin, P. N., & Västfjäll, D. (2008). Emotional responses to music: the need to consider underlying mechanisms. The Behavioral and brain sciences, 31(5), 559–75; discussion 575–621. doi:10.1017/S0140525X08005293

Juslin, P. N., & Västfjäll, D. (2010). How does music evoke emotions? Exploring the underlying mechanisms. In P. N. Juslin & J. A. Sloboda (Eds.), Handbook of music and emotion: Theory, research, applications (pp. 223–253). Oxford: Oxford University Press.

Lantos, G. P., & Craton, L. G. (2012). A model of consumer response to advertising music. Journal of Consumer Marketing, 29(1), 22–42.

Meyer, L. B. (1956). Emotion And Meaning In Music. Chicago: The University Of Chicago Press.

North, A. C., & Hargreaves, D. J. (2008). The Social and Applied Psychology of Music. Oxford: Oxford University Press.

Scherer, K. R. (1999). Appraisal Theory. In T. Dalgleish & M. Power (Eds.), Handbook of cognition and emotion (pp. 637–663). Wiley.

Scherer, K. R. (2005). What are Emotions? And how can they be measured? Social Science Information, 44(4), 695-729.

Scherer, K. R., & Zentner, M. R. (2001). Emotional effects of music: Production rules. In P. N. Juslin & J. A. Sloboda (Eds.), Music and emotion: Theory and research (pp. 361-392). Oxford: Oxford University Press.

Steinbeis, N., Koelsch, S., & Sloboda, J. A. (2006). The Role of Harmonic Expectancy Violations in Musical Emotions : Evidence from Subjective , Physiological , and Neural Responses. Journal of Cognitive Neuroscience, 1380–1393.

Vermeulen, I., Hartmann, T., Welling, A.-M. (2011). The Chill Factor: Improving Ad Responses by Employing Chill-Inducing Background Music. Proceedings of the 61th Annual Conference of the International Communication Association (ICA), May 26-30, Boston, MA.

Zander, M. F. (2006). Musical influences in advertising: how music modifies first impressions of product endorsers and brands. Psychology of Music, 34(4), 465–480.

Multisensory Augmented Reality in the Context of a Retail Clothing Application

Cristy Ho[1], Russ Jones[2], Scott King[2], Lynne Murray[3], & Charles Spence[1]

1 Crossmodal Research Laboratory, Department of Experimental Psychology, University of Oxford, Oxford, UK
2 Condiment Junkie, London, UK
3 Holition, London, UK

Key Words

augmented reality, presence, multisensory perception, clothing, naturalistic product sounds, texture

Abstract

A growing body of research now shows that, across a variety of application domains, the more senses that a virtual reality (VR) application s(t)imulates, the more immersive the experience for the user. That is, the more multisensory the interface, the more immersive it is, the greater the sense of presence that is likely to be experienced by the user (see Gallace et al., 2012, for a recent review). In the present study, we investigated whether augmented reality (AR) clothing experiences could also be made more immersive (i.e., if we could increase the amount of time that people would spend interacting with the system) simply by adding realistic auditory feedback to what has traditionally always been a purely unimodal visual experience. The participants in the present study interacted with an AR clothing display that either operated in silence or else presented movement-locked realistic auditory feedback (consisting of high-quality recordings of the sounds of the two different tested garments being touched). It was found that people interacted with the system for significantly longer (30%) and they were also willing to pay more for the jacket that they experienced in the presence of realistic sounds than in silence.

1. Introduction

The last few years has witnessed growing excitement associated with the utilization of augmented reality (AR) in the context of enhancing the experience of shoppers (e.g., Dredge, 2012). One area of particular interest in recent years relates to the opportunity that such technologies enable clothing stores to allow their customers to see what a particular item of clothing would look like on them, even if that item, colour, size, or style should happen to be unavailable in store at the time of the customer's visit (BBC Newsbeat, 2011). Those with an eye on the future of clothing/retail (e.g., Quinn, 2012) are confidently predicting that such new technologies are going to revolutionize (some might even say revitalize) the retail sector in the face of increasing online competition (e.g., see Spence & Gallace, 2011).

However, to date the majority of examples of AR in a retail context have been strictly unimodal. That is, the users may indeed be able see themselves wearing an item of clothing, but they have been unable to smell the garment, feel it, nor can they hear the texture as they touch it (or move while wearing it). Research in the field of multisensory perception suggests that this lack of realistic multisensory input is likely to diminish the shopper's experience, because our experience of many products, and clothing is no exception here, is genuinely multisensory. Indeed, there is a growing body of laboratory-based research out there demonstrating just how important the sight, the feel (Guest & Spence, 2003a, b; Spence & Gallace, 2011), the sound (Guest et al., 2002; Spence, 2011), and even the fragrance (Demattè et al., 2006; Spence, 2008) associated with an item of clothing can be to influencing a person's perception of, and interaction with, an item of apparel (see also Balla, 1973; Churchill et al., 2009; Fiore, 1993, Fiore, Yah, & Yoh, 2000; Hirsch, 1990;

Spangenberg et al., 2006; Spence & Zampini, 2006). Intriguingly, other research groups are already starting to work in this area, that is, they are trying to figure out how to add realistic sound to virtual clothing (Steele, 2012).

We therefore conducted a preliminary experiment in order to evaluate the claim that adding realistic auditory feedback associated with a person touching, or moving in, the item of clothing shown virtually in the AR setup would enhance the experience of the end user (e.g., the person out shopping for clothes).

2. Methods

2.1 Participants

Twelve participants (8 women, 4 men, mean age of 26 years, age range 20-32 years) took part in the study.

2.2 Apparatus and Materials

The virtual clothing simulation setup consisted of a Kinect Sensor for Xbox 360 (Microsoft, USA), a PC computer (Dell, UK), a 40" LCD screen (NEC, UK; 1920 × 1080 pixels resolution; 60 Hz refresh rate), and a pair of cordless stereo headphones (Philips, UK). The simulation was generated by the Virtual Clothing R&D 0.0.2 software (Holition, UK).

The simulation consisted of an AR environment in which three winter jackets were displayed on the left margin (side) of the display (see **Figure 1**). The user's own face and body was captured by the camera and displayed at the centre of the display, as if they were looking at themselves in the mirror. Upon selection of one of the three jackets, the user was shown wearing the virtual jacket. The user was then free to make any body movement they liked while wearing the virtual jacket.

Audio recordings of the actual garments featured in the simulation were made by Condiment Junkie, UK using a Sennheiser 416 shotgun microphone placed next to the moving arm to record close movements, and a Rode NT-4 stereo microphone in front of the body.

Figure 1. A shot of a user interacting with the virtual clothing simulation. The user is shown trying on a white jacket (not tested in the experiment) in the augmented reality environment. Insert on bottom right shows the user wearing his actual clothing.

The recordings from the Sennheiser microphone were biased towards the relevant side in the stereo field, that is, left arm panned to the left. The Rode microphone in front remained centred. This provided the most realistic stereo replication of someone moving their own arm as they wore one of the jackets. The movement of both arms were recorded separately, swinging from front to back and back to front, at slow, medium, and fast speeds.

2.3 Design and Procedure

The participants were told to imagine that they were out shopping for a winter jacket and trying on two options (the blue and red jackets) in the virtual clothing simulation, one with sound and the other in silence (counterbalanced across participants). We measured how long each participant interacted with the system while trying on the jacket in each condition. At the end, we asked which jacket they were more likely to buy and the price they would be willing to pay for each jacket. The order in which the participants tried on the two jackets, and the two sound conditions, were counterbalanced across participants.

3. Results

The results revealed that participants spent significantly more time while trying on a virtually jacket with realistic clothing sounds (M = 16.3 s) than when no sound was presented (M = 12.0 s), $t(11) = 2.23$, p = .045). This means that adding the multisensory clothing sounds increased the amount of time that people spent interacting with the setup by more than a third. This result is consistent with the claim that the experience of virtually trying on the clothes was much more immersive when sound was presented.

The analysis of the data revealed no evidence of order effects: That is, it did not seem to matter whether the first jacket that the participant tried on came with the realistic clothing sounds or not, $t(11) = 1.11, p = .29$.

Participants were willing to pay more for the jacket experienced with auditory feedback (M = £64) than for the jacket tried on in silence (M = £57), although this trend failed to reach statistical significance, $t(11) = 1.20, p = .25$. (It would obviously be especially interesting to repeat this study with a larger number of participants in order to determine whether this commercially relevant finding would reach statistical significance with a larger N.)

All but one of the participants eventually chose the blue jacket.

4. Conclusions

The results of the experiment reported here provide some of the first evidence to suggest that adding realistic clothing sounds to an AR clothing interface can give rise to a significantly more immersive experience (as suggested by the longer period of time that participants spent trying on the virtual item of clothing when their interactions with the system resulted in the presentation of realistic clothing sounds). This finding is consistent with a variety of previous research findings showing the beneficial effects of adding additional sensory modalities of input to a variety of VR applications (see Gallace et al., 2012, for a recent review).

The results of the present study should, however, be taken as preliminary. In particular, it is impossible to say on the basis of the results reported here how close a match is actually needed between the visually-perceived texture of the AR garment and the sounds that participants heard in order to deliver a multisensory AR experience that consumers find pleasant (or realistic). It should also be noted that precisely synchronizing the visual and auditory feedback in the present setup proved technically challenging. Nevertheless, our results do suggest a number of intriguing directions for future research, including assessing how the multisensory experience of AR clothing would change, and could perhaps be enhanced, by playing back clothing sounds designed to emphasize a particular tactile attribute of the clothing, such as, for example, its softness or smoothness (see Guest et al., 2002; Spence, 2011; Spence & Zampini, 2006).

Of course, for an actual retail application, it is highly unlikely that a shopper would be wearing headphones. However, we would expect the same pattern of results to be obtained should a loudspeaker have been used to present the sounds, rather than wireless headphones. In the future, it would be interesting to use either a flat panel loudspeaker or even a hyper-directional loudspeaker in order to target the clothing sounds (or any other auditory stimulus) direct to the person who is interacting with the AR application.

From a more research-based perspective, it would also be interesting to see whether people's behaviour changes as a function of the virtual clothing they happen to see (and possibly hear) themselves wearing, given the latest research findings showing that people's behaviour sometimes changes when they change the clothes that they are wearing (Adam & Galinsky, 2012).

It would also be of interest in future research to investigate whether adding the appropriate background soundscape could enhance the buying intent of a potential customer, or the price that a customer is willing to pay for a particular item – just think of the sound of a howling gale when trying on a winter jacket, or the sound of the waves gently lapping against the sandy shoreline when trying on a virtual bikini. One could also imagine playing the brand sound and/or signature sound associated with a particular retail experience (just think of the distinctive sound of Abercrombie & Fitch audio mixes here).

References

Adam, H., & Galinsky, A. D. (2012). Enclothed cognition. Journal of Experimental Social Psychology, 48, 918-925.

Balla, G. (1973). Futurist manifesto of men's clothing 1913. In U. Apollonio (ed.), Futurist Manifestos, pp. 132-135. New York: Viking.

BBC Newsbeat (2011, Nov 9). Virtual mirror set to hit clothes shops. (http://www.bbc.co.uk/newsbeat/15640452; accessed on 27/10/12)

Churchill, A., Meyners, M., Griffiths, L., & Bailey, P. (2009). The cross-modal effect of fragrance in shampoo: Modifying the perceived feel of both product and hair during and after washing. Food Quality and Preference, 20, 320-328.

Dematté, M. L., Sanabria, D., Sugarman, R., & Spence, C. (2006). Cross-modal interactions between olfaction and touch. Chemical Senses, 31, 291-300.

Dredge, S. (2012, August 2). IBM aims at retailers with augmented reality shopping app. The Guardian. (http://www.guardian.co.uk/technology/appsblog/2012/aug/02/ibm-augmented-reality-shopping-app; downloaded on 27/10/12)

Fiore, A. M. (1993). Multisensory integration of visual, tactile, and olfactory aesthetic cues of appearance. Clothing and Textile Research Journal, 11, 45-52.

Fiore, A. M., Yah, X., & Yoh, E. (2000). Effects of a product display and environmental fragrancing on approach responses and pleasurable experiences. Psychology & Marketing, 17, 27-54.

Gallace, A., Ngo, M. K., Sulaitis, J., & Spence, C. (2012). Multisensory presence in virtual reality: Possibilities & limitations. In G. Ghinea, F. Andres, & S. Gulliver (eds.), Multiple sensorial media advances and applications: New developments in MulSeMedia, pp. 1-40. IGI Global.

Guest, S., Catmur, C., Lloyd, D., & Spence, C. (2002). Audiotactile interactions in roughness perception. Experimental Brain Research, 146, 161-171.

Guest, S., & Spence, C. (2003a). Tactile dominance in speeded discrimination of pilled fabric samples. Experimental Brain Research, 150, 201-207.

Guest, S., & Spence, C. (2003b). What role does multisensory integration play in the visuotactile perception of texture? International Journal of Psychophysiology, 50, 63-80.

Hirsch, A. R. (1990). Preliminary results of olfaction Nike study, note dated November 16 distributed by the Smell and Taste Treatment and Research Foundation, Ltd. Chicago, IL.

Quinn, B. (2012). Fashion futures. London: Merrell.

Spangenberg, E. R., Sprott, D. E., Grohmann, B., & Tracy, D. L. (2006). Gender-congruent ambient scent influences on approach and avoidance behaviors in a retail store. Journal of Business Research, 59, 1281-1287.

Spence, C. (2008). Sensing the future. In L. Miles (ed.), AQR directory & handbook 2008, pp. 56-60. St. Neots, Cambridgeshire: AQR.

Spence, C. (2011). Sound design: How understanding the brain of the consumer can enhance auditory and multisensory product/brand development. In K. Bronner, R. Hirt, & C. Ringe (eds.), Audio Branding Academy Yearbook 2010/2011, pp. 35-49. Baden-Baden, Germany: Nomos Verlag.

Spence, C., & Gallace, A. (2011). Multisensory design: Reaching out to touch the consumer. Psychology & Marketing, 28, 267-308.

Spence, C., & Zampini, M. (2006). Auditory contributions to multisensory product perception. Acta Acustica united with Acustica, 92, 1009-1025.

Steele, B. (2012). Scientists simulate clothing sounds for computer animation. Cornell University Chronicle Online (http://www.news.cornell.edu/stories/Sept12/ClothSounds.html; downloaded on 26/10/12)

"Hot or Cold?" On the Informative Value of Auditory Cues in the Perception of the Temperature of a Beverage

Carlos Velasco[1], Russ Jones[2], Scott King[2], & Charles Spence[1]

1 Crossmodal Research Laboratory, Department of Experimental Psychology, University of Oxford, Oxford, UK
2 Condiment Junkie, London, UK

Key Words

crossmodal correspondences, temperature, product sounds, sonic design, product design

Abstract

We conducted a study designed to assess whether people can discriminate between the sounds made by hot and cold liquids when poured into various drinking vessels. The results of an initial questionnaire revealed that, on average, only half of the people we asked thought that this would be possible. However, the results of a subsequent experiment in which participants had to classify 6 pre-recorded liquid pouring sounds (the sounds of hot and cold water being poured into three different receptacles: a glass, a porcelain cup, and a paper cup) as either 'hot' or 'cold' revealed that people are actually surprisingly good at this task. Our participants were able to discriminate the temperature of the liquid (e.g., hot or cold) on the basis of the auditory cues at a level that was significantly better than chance (M = 72% correct, on average). These results therefore suggest that people really can hear the temperature of a drink being poured. A number of ideas for the future commercialization of such results are discussed.

1. Introduction

Most of the information that we process from the environment is multisensory in nature. Furthermore, the information we get from each of the senses is often interrelated both at perceptual and semantic levels. Perhaps unsurprisingly, marketers have, in recent years, started to become increasingly interested in figuring out how to enhance the multisensory properties of the products/services that they promote, and how those enhanced multisensory product properties can then beneficially impact upon consumer perception and behaviour (e.g., Krishna, 2012; Spence, 2012).

The last few years have seen a rapid growth of interest from both academic researchers and sonic branding practitioners concerning how to quantify the impact of auditory cues on the consumer's multisensory experience of both products and services. The ultimate aim here has been to enhance the customer experience of a given product or service (see Spence, 2012; Spence & Shankar, 2010, for reviews). One of the best-known examples of sonic design is the sound of the car engine (e.g., Spence & Zampini, 2006). It is certainly true that the automotive sector has been one of the most consistently well-funded areas for sonic design research in recent decades; just think about everything from the sound of the car engine through to the satisfying clunk of the car door closing. This trend shows every sign of continuing given that many of the car companies are now turning their attention to the optimal sound for the electric cars that will increasingly come to dominate our roads in the years to come (e.g., Bergeron, Astruc, & Masson, 2010; Miśkiewicz & Letowski, 1999).

Intriguingly, the ideas and insights that were originally perfected in the automotive sector are now increasingly being extended/applied to a variety of other product categories. After all, the majority of our product interactions generate auditory feedback, and those sounds influence our perception, no matter whether we realize it or not (and mostly, we do not, see Spence, 2012). Researchers have demonstrated the effect that modifying the sound can have on people's perception of the pleasantness of everyday products as diverse as electric toothbrushes (Zampini,

Guest & Spence, 2003) and aerosol sprays (Spence & Zampini, 2007), through to crisp packets (Spence, 2013) and coffee makers (Knöferle, 2012).

The auditory cues that happen to be associated with the use of a variety of everyday products can provide a rich source of information for customers/consumers. For instance, Byron (2012) recently described a number of examples of companies who have utilized sonic design in order to enhance consumer perception of their products. They include the Dr Pepper Snapple Group Inc., who highlights the distinctive sound (the "*Snapple pop*") of *Snapple* bottles when first opened; such signature sounds certainly have the potential to set consumer expectations. Or take Dyson. They have been working on making their vacuum cleaners sound more pleasant when operational since the company is sure that consumers are influenced by such product sounds. Fenko, Schifferstein and Hekkert (2011) recently demonstrated that the perceived noisiness and annoyance of products such as alarm clocks and whistling kettles was primarily influenced by their auditory (as compared to visual) features. These researchers went on to argue that product sounds need to be taken more seriously when it comes to multisensory product design (see also Wolkomir, 1996).

It is important to note that auditory cues can also exert a profound impact on our perception of many food and drink products as well. In a recent review, Spence (2012) highlighted how most of the studies that have been published in this area to date have tended to focus on the influence of sounds (associated with eating behaviours and food) on food evaluation and taste/flavour perception, not to mention on the influence of background noise on food experiences/behaviours. Meanwhile, Zampini and Spence (2005) demonstrated that people's perception of the carbonation of a fizzy drink held in the hand could be modified significantly simply by changing the 'popping' sounds that people hear (either boosting or cutting certain frequency components and/or speeding-up the popping sounds).

Modifying what a consumer hears can, then, be used to influence their perception of many different products and brands (see Byron, 2012; Spence & Zampini, 2006). Such sonic design may be so successful precisely because of the fact that the sounds that result from our interaction with the environment convey relevant information of the nature of objects with which we are interacting (e.g., Gaver, 1993; Giordano & McAdams, 2006). However, further research is still needed in order to clarify exactly how sonic cues influence our perception of certain other object properties. Take, for example, the sound that a liquid makes when poured into a receptacle, it will likely depend both on the material properties of the receptacle (a paper cup will sound very different to porcelain, say) and on the temperature of the liquid itself (hot vs. cold; e.g., Parthasarathy & Chhapga, 1955).

That said, how exactly would you describe the difference between the sound of a liquid being poured into a cup, for example, a hot cup of coffee or a cold glass of water? Would it be possible, do you think, to discriminate whether that liquid was hot or cold on the basis of its sound? To the best of our knowledge, there are, as yet, no well-controlled empirical studies that have attempted to assess the relationship between the sound of pouring and temperature perception in beverages. To date, the only evidence on this question comes from an anecdotal report mentioned in passing in Barb Stuckey's (2012) recent book, 'Taste what you're missing'. There she states that people can easily discriminate between hot and cold liquid pouring sounds (see also http://www.barbstuckey.com/, accessed on 20/10/12).

We would argue that there is clearly a potential opportunity here for food and beverage development in taking into account different auditory parameters in a range of features like, for example, brand name, packaging sounds, and product sounds, in order to set the consumer's multisensory product expectations more successfully (see Spence, 2011a). In other words, auditory cues may contribute to the creation of expectations in the mind of the consumer regarding the sensory properties (and not just the auditory properties) and attributes of food and drinks. Companies may be able to use such knowledge in order to convey relevant information auditorily (e.g., Ngo et al., 2013) since, very often, our expectations provide a powerful cue to what we, in fact, ultimately end up experiencing (see Schifferstein, 2001).

In the present study we therefore investigated whether the sounds elicited when a liquid is poured into a receptacle do provide sufficient information with which to discern the temperature of a drink. We conducted a preliminary questionnaire, in which participants were asked whether they thought that they could tell if a liquid is hot or cold simply by listening to the sound it made. In a subsequent experiment, we then assessed whether people could actually discriminate between the temperature of a liquid (hot vs. cold) solely on the basis of the sound it made when poured.

2. Preliminary Questionnaire

60 participants (28 males and 32 females) aged 19-60 years (mean= 28.3, SD= 7.5) completed an online questionnaire created with Google Docs' Forms. This is an app that allows one to create online questionnaires and surveys. Participants were asked the following question: *"Do you think that you could tell whether a liquid was hot or cold simply by the sound it made when poured into a receptacle?"* The participants could either answer yes or no. An invitation to complete the questionnaire was distributed electronically to a database of 820 people on Facebook and 1273 on Twitter. 29 participants (48%) responded in the affirmative (that is, they thought that they would be able to discriminate between a hot and a cold drink based solely on the liquid pouring sounds). Thus, the respondents were pretty evenly split in terms of their response to this question.

3. Study

Methods

Twenty eight new participants (17 female and 11 male) from the UK were presented with the sounds of six liquids, three hot and three cold. Audio recordings of the two liquids (hot and cold) being poured into a glass container, a porcelain cup, and a paper cup were made (see **Figure 1**).

Figure 1. Containers into which the hot and cold liquids were poured: A) Glass, B) Porcelain, and C) Paper.

In the experiment, participants were presented with each of the sounds and were instructed to mark on a pencil-and-paper questionnaire whether each liquid sounded hot or cold. The sounds were recorded by Condiment Junkie (London, UK), using a Sennheiser 416 directional shotgun microphone, by pouring 200ml of water into each vessel at around 1 inch above its edge. The cold liquids were fresh out of the fridge at a temperature of 6-8 ºC while the hot liquids were recently boiled at a temperature of 82-84 ºC. The 6 sounds were presented in the following order: (temperature/material): 1) Cold/glass; 2) Hot/glass; 3) Hot/porcelain; 4) Cold/porcelain; 5) Hot/paper; and 6) Cold/paper.

4. Results

A Pearson's Chi Square test (Agresti & Finlay, 2009) was performed on the data in order to determine the association between hot and cold responses and the sounds that were presented: Significant results were observed, $X^2=40.19$, df=5, p<.001, suggesting the existence of an association between the variables. Further analysis included a significance test for proportions to assess whether the majority of the participants chose hot or cold when listening to each of the recordings (see **Figure 2**).

According to the significance test for proportions, the participants were able to discriminate the temperature of the liquids at a level that was significantly better than chance (both p<.05), when the hot and cold sounds were poured into both glass and porcelain.

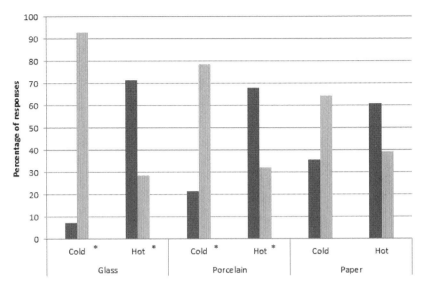

Figure 2. Percentage of hot (dark gray) and cold (light gray) responses for each sound as a function of the real temperature of the liquids and the materials of the receptacles into which they were poured. * = p= .05 significant difference in likelihood of participants making one of two responses.

These results demonstrate how certain sounds convey potentially useful information to a consumer regarding the temperature of a liquid being poured into a drinking vessel. The results also highlight the fact that people find it rather more difficult to determine the temperature of the drink when hot and cold liquids are poured in paper containers (although a trend in the right direction could nevertheless still be seen in the data). Taken together, these results suggest that people's ability to discriminate the temperature of liquids may, in part, depend on the material properties of the containers into which they happen to be poured.

5. Discussion

The results reported here provide some of the first empirical support for the claim that people can discriminate the temperature of a beverage solely of the basis of the auditory cues that the liquid makes when poured into a drinking vessel (e.g., a cup or glass). Interestingly, however, the information contained in such liquid pouring sounds seems not to be consciously recognized by many people – at least if the results of our preliminary online questionnaire are anything to go by. The results reported here are, though, consistent with anecdotal reports concerning people's ability to discriminate the temperature of liquid pouring sounds (see Stuckey, 2012).

Our findings are entirely consistent with previous findings suggesting that the perception of temperature is multisensory. For example, Fenko, Schifferstein, and Hekkert (2010) reported three experiments in which they assessed how colour and materials influence people's experience of the warmth of products (specifically, scarves and breakfast trays), by presenting either visual or tactile stimuli. Both the colours and materials of the products were found to be equally important when it came to conveying information about the warmth of the product. Meanwhile, Wastiels, Schifferstein, Heylighen, and Wouters (2012) reported that both the colour and roughness of a material can influence perceived warmth. Taken together, these results therefore suggest that the perception of warmth may be a multisensory construct – one that is based primarily on tactile inputs, but which can also be influenced by cues from many of the other senses as well.

It is possible to imagine a wide range of potential applications for the findings reported here: Everything from 'enhancing' (or emphasizing) the apparent temperature (e.g., hot or cold) of a beverage in a radio or television commercial (e.g., for a tea brand, say; see Spence, 2011a, b) through to improving the auditory qualities of electronic drinks dispensers, not to mention other household appliances (see Knöferle, 2011; Spence & Zampini, 2006). In the future, one could even imagine a range of intriguing dishes in modernist restaurants (such as, perhaps, variants on the "*Hot and iced tea*" served at The Fat Duck restaurant in Bray; see Blumenthal, 2008) where sensory incongruity is used – e.g., so that a dish that the diner expects to be hot is actually served (poured) cold or vice versa (see Piqueras-Fiszman & Spence, 2012, for a review of the use of sensory incongruity in the gastronomy and food sectors).

Carlos Velasco, Russ Jones, Scott King, Charles Spence

During our everyday interactions, we often see steam rising from the surface of a food or beverage product (e.g., imagine a freshly poured hot cup of tea). People presumably normally use such visual cues in order to guide their estimates (or expectancy) concerning the drink's likely temperature. One particularly interesting question for future research will therefore be to investigate what happens when such visual cues to the temperature of a food or beverage are placed into conflict with the temperature of the sound of that product (be it a hot or cold drink being poured into a receptacle, as here, or the sizzle of the hot plate as the waiter brings the steak to your table; see Wheeler, 1938).

Which sense dominates under such conditions of intersensory conflict is an open question: However, if one was to hazard a guess, and based on a variety of research published in the area to date, the likely answer is that vision would dominate over audition (Spence, 2011b). Even if that were to be the case, though, one could imagine a number of intriguing drinks that could nevertheless still be served in the context of the currently popular dine-in-the-dark restaurants (see Spence & Piqueras-Fiszman, 2012) where sensory incongruity (or surprise) could be elicited by serving a cold drink after the diner has heard what sounds like a hot drink being poured (Piqueras-Fiszman & Spence, 2012).

To conclude, while most people believe that hot and cold are primarily thermal properties, based on tactile (and/or oral-somatosensory) inputs to the skin, in fact, like many other attributes, the consumer's perception of this quality can be modulated by means of the (sometimes subtle) cues presented to the other senses as well. In the future, it will be particularly interesting to use a simplified variant of the Implicit Association Test (IAT; e.g., see Demattè, Sanabria, & Spence, 2007; Greenwald, McGhee, & Schwartz, 1998; Parise & Spence, 2012) in order to determine whether such liquid pouring sounds are automatically and implicitly associated with the notion of a particular temperature (or at the very least with a distinction between hot and cold beverages). One could even imagine creating caricatured sounds that enhance the perceived temperature of a drink product that could be used to enhance the multisensory appeal of a product or brand. It would also be very interesting to see whether changing the 'temperature' of pouring sounds would also change the perceived temperature of a drink for consumers.

Acknowledgements

Our thanks to Colebrooke Row and Zoe Burgess of The Drink Factory for helping out with the research reported here. Carlos Velasco would also like to thank COLFUTURO, Colombia, for funding his PhD.

References

Agresti, A., & Finlay, B. (2009). Statistical methods for the social sciences (4th Ed.). New Jersey: Pearson Prentice Hall.

Bergeron, F., Astruc, C., & Masson, P. (2010). Sound quality assessment of internal automotive road noise using sensory science. Acta Acustica united with Acustica, 96, 580-588.

Blumenthal, H. (2008). The big Fat Duck cookbook. London: Bloomsbury.

Byron, E. (2012). The search for sweet sounds that sell: Household products' clicks and hums are no accident; Light piano music when the dishwasher is done? The Wall Street Journal, October 23, downloaded on 02/11/12 from http://online.wsj.com/article/SB1000142405297020340640457807467 15 98804116.html?mod=googlenews_wsj#articleTabs%3Darticle

Demattè, M. L., Sanabria, D., & Spence, C. (2007). Olfactory-tactile compatibility effects demonstrated using the implicit association task. Acta Psychologica, 124, 332-343.

Fenko, A., Schifferstein, H. N. J., & Hekkert, P. (2010). Looking hot or feeling hot: What determines the product experience of warmth? Materials & Design, 31, 1325-1331.

Fenko, A., Schifferstein, H. N. J., & Hekkert, P. (2011). Noisy products: Does appearance matter? International Journal of Design, 5(3), 77-87.

Gaver, W. W. (1993). What in the world do we hear? An ecological approach to auditory event perception. Ecological Psychology, 5, 1-29.

Giordano, B. L., & McAdams, S. (2006). Material identification of real impact sounds: Effects of size variation in steel, glass, wood, and plexiglass plates. Journal of the Acoustical Society of America, 119, 1171-1181.

Greenwald, A. G., McGhee, D. E., & Schwartz, J. L. K. (1998). Measuring individual differences in implicit cognition: The implicit association test. Journal of Personality and Social Psychology, 74, 1464-1480.

Knöferle, K. M. (2012). Using customer insights to improve product sound design. Marketing Review St. Gallen, 29, 47-53.

Krishna, A. (2012). An integrative review of sensory marketing: Engaging the senses to affect perception, judgment and behavior. Journal of Consumer Psychology, 22, 332-351.

Miśkiewicz, A., & Letowski, T. (1999). Psychoacustics in the automotive industry. Acta Acustica united with Acustica, 85, 646-649.

Ngo, M. K., Velasco, C., Salgado, A., Boehm, E., O'Neill, D., & Spence, C. (2013). Assessing crossmodal correspondences in exotic fruit juices: The case of shape and sound symbolism. Food Quality and Preference, 28, 361-369.

Parise, C. V., & Spence, C. (2012). Assessing the associations between brand packaging and brand attributes using an indirect performance measure. Food Quality and Preference, 24, 17-23.

Parthasarathy, S., & Chhapga, A. F. (1955). Sound absorption in liquids in relationship to their physical properties: Viscosity and specific heats. Annalen der Physik, 5, 297-303.

Piqueras-Fiszman, B., & Spence, C. (2012). Sensory incongruity in the food and beverage sector: Art, science, and commercialization. Petits Propos Culinaires, 95, 74-118.

Schifferstein, H. N. J. (2001). Effects of product beliefs on product perception and liking. In L. Frewer, E. Risvik, & H. Schifferstein (Eds.), Food, people and society: A European perspective of consumers' food choices (pp. 73-96). Berlin: Springer Verlag.

Spence, C. (2011a). Managing sensory expectations concerning products and brands: Capitalizing on the potential of sound and shape symbolism. Journal of Consumer Psychology, 22, 37-54.

Spence, C. (2011b). Sound design: How understanding the brain of the consumer can enhance auditory and multisensory product/brand development. In K. Bronner, R. Hirt, & C. Ringe (Eds.), Audio Branding Academy Yearbook 2010/2011 (pp. 35-49). Baden-Baden, Germany: Nomos Verlag.

Spence, C. (2012). Auditory contributions to flavour perception and feeding behaviour. Physiology & Behaviour, 107, 505-515.

Spence, C., & Piqueras-Fiszman, B. (2012). Dining in the dark: Why, exactly, is the experience so popular? The Psychologist, 25, 888-891.

Spence, C., & Shankar, M. U. (2010). The influence of auditory cues on the perception of, and responses to, food and drink. Journal of Sensory Studies, 25, 406-430.

Spence, C., & Zampini, M. (2006). Auditory contributions to multisensory product perception. Acta Acustica united with Acustica, 92, 1009-1025.

Spence, C., & Zampini, M. (2007). Affective design: Modulating the pleasantness and forcefulness of aerosol sprays by manipulating aerosol spraying sounds. CoDesign: International Journal of CoCreation in Design and the Arts, 3, 107-121.

Stuckey, B. (2012). Taste what you're missing: The passionate eater's guide to why good food tastes good. London: Free Press.

Wastiels, L., Schifferstein, H. N. J., Heylighen, A., & Wouters, I. (2012). Red or rough, what makes materials warmer? Materials and Design, 43, 441-449.

Wheeler, E. (1938). Tested sentences that sell. New York: Prentice & Co.

Wolkomir, R. (1996). Decibel by decibel, reducing the din to a very dull roar. Smithsonian Magazine, February, 56-65.

Zampini, M., Guest, S., & Spence, C. (2003). The role of auditory cues in modulating the perception of electric toothbrushes. Journal of Dental Research, 82, 929-932.

Zampini, M., & Spence, C. (2005). Modifying the multisensory perception of a carbonated beverage using auditory cues. Food Quality and Preference, 16, 632-641.

Particularities and Differences in the Creation Process of Sound Branding by Sound Branders and Other Professional Composers

Evelyn Kreb, Diana Tobias, Stephanie Forge

University of Paderborn

Key Words

creation process, approach, creativity, professional distinction, popular music composition

Abstract

As a complex interaction of creativity and expertise, the creation process of sound branding has not been examined so far. This study seeks to unravel the approaches, proceedings and characteristic features of professional sound branders. In order to do so, methodologically, the particularities of the sound branding creation process are elaborated by a comparison with the proceeding in the composition of "non-functional" music. For this purpose, four expert interviews were carried out with two sound branders and two other professional composers.

Analysing the interview contents, different strategies, representations and musically creative approaches toward the creation of sound branding become obvious. Being part of the interviews, an outstanding experiment shows similarities between the two professions, though, and is able to point out that sound branding could become a field of working for professional composers of other music as well.

1. Introduction

Sound branding is one part of the creation of a brand image and corporate design that has gained importance in the targeted designing of brand communication since its first establishment as an independent department in marketing agencies at the turn of the past century.

In contrast to this, scientific research has hardly been paying attention to this phenomenon for a long time. The small number of publications mostly consists of descriptions of its positive effects for a company, as sound branding can improve the recognition factor of companies, brands and products and thereby lead to a competitive advantage (cf. Kastner, 2008, p. 36; Steiner, 2009, p. 53). Furthermore, the historical development, the aims and criteria of sound branding were explained by Kai Bronner and Rainer Hirt (2007) who also make first descriptive approaches towards the creation process.

Nevertheless, due to the complex cooperation structures and the ways of proceeding of the individual participants involved, the sound branding creation process still appears obscure. To fill these gaps in scientific research, this study is going to find out if there are particularities in the creation process of sound branding by comparing it to conventional ways of composing.

The main emphasis is put on the elements of the creative process a composer goes through, in particular the "translation" of brand and product characteristics into tonal attributes. This concerns for example the parameters used, the formal structure or potential technical aids.

The hypotheses for this study were:

- Sound branders can "translate" the characteristics, verbalized attributively by the client, more easily and thereby more quickly into an acoustic interpretation than other professional composers.
- Sound branders, who follow a rather functional and targeted approach, concentrate on the functional service aspect of their work aiming for a means of image creation for the client. The other professional composers, working more associatively and

musically-creatively, give the priority to their own aesthetic ideas.

- Sound branders will use product sounds, speech or other sound-oriented means of designing, whereas other professional composers will mostly use melodic and rhythmic elements.

2. Method

As the topic is still unexplored, the starting point of this case study is a qualitative approach to gain new results concerning the questions:

1. What characterises the sound branding creation process in contrast to other composing?
2. What competences does a sound brander need?
3. Would other professional composers be able to work in this field, too?

To answer these questions, four expert interviews were lead with a partly standardized way of questioning and an experimental part.

Interview partners and situations

The interviews took place in 2011, three of them were in-person interviews, one was conducted via the Internet phone service "Skype". All respondents were male, aged 23 to 50, and they spent voluntarily 60 to 90 minutes answering the questions of the same two interviewers.

The four experts were chosen in reference to Alexander Bogner et al. (2002) who claim that the knowledge of experts *"comprises complexly integrated states of knowledge and is furthermore constitutively related to the practising of their professions"* (Bogner et al., 2002, p. 4)[1]. The first interview was conducted with a sound brander, called Sound-Brander1, via "Skype". He finished his studies of Music and Media in 2008, was a trainee in a sound branding agency and has been working as a freelance composer for advertising and pop music ever since.

---

1 Original citation in German. Translated by the authors.

The second interview with a sound brander took place in the recording studio of SoundBrander2, composer and sound engineer who creates and produces sound design, music for advertising and TV spots.

The third interview took place in a café with a composer, called Composer1, who is studying integrative composition pop/jazz. He writes music of various genres, for example big band style, ballads or music for theatre projects, and claims to not have any experience in the creation of sound branding.

The last interview partner was a composer, Composer2, who was interviewed in his office. He is a musician and mostly writes pieces in the style of chansons, soul, jazz and stage music. He has never been involved in sound branding so far.

Interview structure

For the problem-focused interviews, a manual was developed that was supposed to both structure the conversation and still keep it open for new impulses. Moreover, the interview should *take a natural course, for which the interview partner can choose the order of the topics, too".* (Kastner, 2008, p. 93)[2]

The following list shows some of the numerous questions that were classified under four major topics:

A) Definition of sound branding
   "How do you define sound branding?"
   "Do you know what sound branding is?"

B) Creation process of sound branding
   "Do you feel your creativity is restricted by guidelines?"
   "Do/would you use 'classic parameters'?"

C) Composition process of other music
   "Do/would you use 'classic' parameters?"
   "How do you proceed when you compose other music?"

---

2   Original citation in German. Translated by the authors.

D) Demographic data

"What type of education do you have?"

"Since when do you practise your profession?"

To improve the understanding of the creation process by a "real" experience, the respondents were asked to "get into action" themselves. Without any further briefing, except for approximative indications concerning price and target group, they should develop ideas for a sound branding for a glass of the brand LEONARDO (cf. **Figure 1**).

Figure 1. LEONARDO glasses (picture courtesy of LEONARDO / glaskoch B. Koch jr. GmbH + Co. KG).

Afterwards, they were asked to explain their individual way of proceeding. The interviews were recorded, transcribed and summarized in the form of theses, which finally were assigned to the major question of the study.

3. Results

3.1 Success factors of a sound branding

The five most important factors for a successful sound branding mentioned by at least two of the respondents were distinctiveness, conformity with product/company, the broadcasting frequency, independence and memorability.

Each one of the four respondents, and thereby both professions, mentioned distinctiveness as a major factor of success. The two composers and SoundBrander2 said that there must be a conformity with the product or the company. SoundBrander2 and Composer1 thought that the broadcasting frequency had an effect on the success of the sound branding. That a sound branding has to be independent was mentioned by the two sound branders, whereas the two composers emphasized the necessity of memorability.

Furthermore, individual answers were made for flexibility, shortness, conciseness, the way of presentation, customer satisfaction, conformity with advertising and marketing as well as conformity with target group preferences.

3.2 Key competences of a sound brander

Mentioned by all respondents, musical flexibility can be called a major necessary characteristic of a sound brander. The sound branders and Composer2 talked about analytical comprehension and technical skills as key qualifications. Selling competence was named by SoundBrander2 and Composer1.

Probably influenced by their experience, both sound branders mentioned flexibility in time, whereas the composers see communicative and social skills as an important characteristic of a sound brander. Apart from these, there were single answers naming creativity, curiosity and the ability to be inspired, the neglect of own preferences as well as thinking economically.

3.3 Approach to the process of creation

The sound branders were asked to describe their usual way of proceeding when they get the commission to create a sound branding. The composers should answer the question how they might probably proceed if they were in such a situation.

During the interviews, four individual approaches became recognizable: First, an intuitive experimental approach, second, a strategic intuitive approach, third, an associative experimental approach and finally, an analytical associative approach.

All the respondents mentioned a market, product, company or target group analysis as a major part for the creation of a suitable sound branding, furthermore, this requires an analysis of parallel advertising activities like visual material, music or marketing.

The two sound branders said that they would consider taking up older ideas, but in one case only under time pressure.

3.4 Similarities and differences to the approach to popular music

Not only the composers but also the sound branders write "non-functional" popular music. Therefore, the (hypothetical) approach to the creation of sound branding was compared to the one to popular music.

The two creation processes have in common that all respondents would enjoy them both. SoundBrander1 and Composer1 agreed that composing popular music offers more flexibility in time. Apart from this, the various answers were very individual and partly contradictory. Concerning the communication with the client, SoundBrander1 claimed it to be more lively when composing popular music, which is also due to less time pressure. Ironically, Composer1 thought it to be more important in the creation process of sound branding.

Moreover, Composer2 claimed an analytical approach to be the basis for the composition of popular music as well as the creation of sound branding, whereas SoundBrander2 states to proceed more analytically when creating sound branding.

3.5 Use of composition tools and other aids

The questioning has shown that in the creation process of sound logos, longer advertising music as well as popular music, sequencer programs would be preferred. They serve as a means for the final production or to record the sound ideas for presenting them to the client. The two composers and SoundBrander2 would begin with a piano for the first steps in the composition of advertising and popular music. In the crea-tion of a sound logo, three of them would use a synthesizer to be able to work with different sounds. For popular music, SoundBrander1 would prefer a guitar and Composer1 would sometimes use a guitar, too.

Other aids like classic rules of composition would be used by two out of four respondents. It is remarkable that the separation is not profession immanent but that one respondent of each profession agrees on using these rules and the other one does not.

An aid like the exchange of ideas with others, for example other composers or sound branders, would be used by all the respondents.

3.6 Potential subjective restriction of creativity due to guiding details

At this point it was necessary to find out if the composers would feel restricted by the existing guiding details from the client in the composition process of sound branding and if the sound branders confirmed or negated such a feeling.

Three of the respondents, of whom the two sound branders and Composer2, said that they would not feel restricted in their creativity by guiding details. However, Composer1 stated that he would experience a certain limitation of his own artistic expression.

3.7 Individual aesthetic views/musical preferences

All the respondents agreed that the customer request was the focus of attention in the creation of a sound branding. The sound branders emphasized that they should limit their own aesthetic ideas or preferences or even try to completely push them in the back of their mind.

Despite this, the two composers as well as SoundBrander2 determine their own musical taste as an indicator for the quality and the suitability of the sound branding, and reveal furthermore that too far-reaching wishes for alteration from the client would restrict their own satisfaction, the identification with their own work and the pleasure of working.

3.8 Suitability of composers for the creation of sound branding

As a last question, the respondents should evaluate if it were possible that composers who have not familiarized themselves with the topic yet, are able to create sound branding. This implies an investigation of the proximity or distance between the two professions and if a strict separation has to be made.

The respondents were divided over this question. SoundBrander2 and Composer1 answered the question in the affirmative but with the reservation that the composers familiarize themselves with the necessary characteristics of a sound branding and working with sounds. The remaining two respondents considered this as essential as well but were more sceptical or even doubted a successful realization. This disagreement makes a clear separation of the two professions impossible.

3.9 Experiment

One outstanding part of the interview was a practical experiment, that was supposed to improve the understanding of the creation process by a "real" experience. The respondents were asked to develop ideas for a sound branding for a glass of the brand LEONARDO (cf. **Figure 1**).

Agreeing to participate in the experiment, the respondents showed a lot of spontaneity and creativity and were all able to create individual concepts for a sound branding. Composer2 even gave a musical demonstration of his idea immediately.

Comparing the developed concepts, astonishing similarities can be remarked. Again they did not arise within the professions but on the contrary, the concepts of each one sound brander and one composer resembled each other:

SoundBrander1 and Composer1 focused on the sound of the glass, the product sound. The two other respondents analysed the final "range of application", the future relationship between the product and the customer and in which context it will be used by the customer. After this, they tried to find a potential affinity of the product with musical ways of expression. Both of them used a piano, in one case with a technically changed sound, in the second case complemented with modern synthesizer sounds. This result proves, even with its experimental background, that a clear separation of the professions or a distinction between the approaches to the creation process of sound branding by sound branders or other professional composers cannot be made.

4. Discussion

This empirical study tried to discover particularities in the creation process of sound branding on the basis of interviews with four experts, two of them sound branders and two other composers. Potentially different views concerning success factors of sound branding, ideas of necessary skills of a sound brander and in particular similarities and differences in the approach towards the creativity process in the creation of sound branding in contrast to other composing were examined. Thereby, the sound branding creation process and its characteristics were unravelled. Analysing the results of the interviews, it became clear that a definite separation concerning the requirements and approaches of the two professions could not be made.

After the analysis, the following statements could be made regarding the hypotheses made at the beginning:

- The experiment showed that with regard to an easier and faster "translation" of verbalized characteristics into an acoustic interpretation, there was no strong difference between sound branders and the other professional composers. All respondents designed a creative concept of musical interpretation of the product attributes in a short amount of time.

- A classification of a functional and targeted approach as belonging to sound branders and an associative, musically creative approach to composers of popular music could not be made. All respondents emphasized the importance of the customer's request. Still, both composers, and this would support the hypothesis, confirmed considering their own aesthetic preferences. But one sound brander did so, too.

- The third hypothesis, which supposed a difference regarding the arrangement and use of musical tools, proved to be only partly true, too. In fact, one sound brander concentrated rather on the product sound and one composer focused on references of the product to musical instruments and parameters. But each second member of the two professions carried out the proceeding expected of the opposed profession. So again, a clear distinction cannot be made as both concepts elaborated during the experiment interpret the product characteristics in a rhythmic and melodic way and use sound as a particular aspect of tonal translation.

Concerning further conclusions and interpretations, certain restrictions of this study have to be considered.

For example, the representativity of the survey is rather limited as only four respondents were interviewed. Therefore, generalizations should only be conditional. Furthermore, the method of the qualitative interviewing structured by a manual but still kept open to a great extent causes asymmetries concerning the contents that were mentioned.

Nevertheless, this proceeding has been chosen intentionally to offer the respondents a large space regarding the main emphases and course of the interviews. Thereby, the main emphasis and the course vary in the individual interviews, different aspects were elaborated in one interview that were only touched upon in the other one.

To define a clear tendency regarding a verification of the hypotheses, the research method should be standardized and the sample extended. Moreover, composers with different musical focuses, for example classical music, should be interviewed to precisely define differences between musical creation processes.

Finally, the concluding statement of all the respondents, that composers may be or are able to create sound branding, too, if they familiarize with the necessary characteristics of a sound branding and working with sounds, is recapitulated.

This statement emphasizes that the two professions are close to each other and that for example a composer could think about using his knowledge and experience in music to work in this field as well.

The study is thereby a first approach toward creative processes in modern fields of composing as well as job characteristics and perspectives for members of the music business.

References

Bogner, A., Littig, B. & Menz, W. (eds.) (2002). Das Experteninterview. Theorie, Methode, Anwendung. [The expert interview. Theory, method and application]. Opladen: Leske und Budrich.

Bronner, K. & Hirt, R. (2007). Audio-Branding. Entwicklung, Anwendung, Wirkung akustischer Identitäten in Werbung, Medien und Gesellschaft. [Audio-Branding. Development, application, effect of acoustic identities in advertising, media and society]. München: Verlag Reinhard Fischer.

Kastner, S. (2008). Klang macht Marken. Sonic Branding als Designprozess. [Sound makes brands. Sonic Branding as design process]. Wiesbaden: GWV Fachverlage GmbH.

Steiner, P. (2009). Sound Branding. Grundlagen der akustischen Markenführung. [Sound Branding. Bases of acoustic branding]. Wiesbaden: GWV Fachverlage GmbH.

The Influence of Sound Design in Videogames on Brand Awareness: An Acoustic Branding Study for MLP and the audio consulting group

Patrick Langeslag[1], Julia Schwieger[1], Martin Sinn[2]

1 audio consulting group, Hamburg
2 Hanze University of Applied Sciences, Groningen

Key Words

acoustic branding, sound logos, sound design, videogames, brand aware-ness

Abstract

The purpose of the report is to assess the influence of sound design in online videogames on user behaviour as well as brand awareness. An online survey (n=149) consisting of four groups has been set up – one control group, one group which was exposed to different sound logos and two groups, which were asked to play a videogame. Both groups played the same game. One of them with non-branded, the other with branded sound design.

The main finding of the report was that sound logos learned in video-games can be connected to a brand. Further, videogames with a branded sound design influence the level of brand recognition positively. More-over, a branded videogames can affect perceived brand values and hence, brand image. Otherwise, the branded sound design had no influ-ence on user behaviour or different aspects of brand awareness.

1. Introduction

1.1 Key Concepts

This study is based on three key concepts – sound design, videogames and acoustic branding.

The term sound design can hereby be defined as the process of creating a desired sound with technical support (Vo, 1994), which has further been supported by Ikonen (2012), who adds time as a relevant factor differentiating sound design from other design areas.

Furthermore, it is necessary to define videogames, in order to see whether the game used for this study can be classified as such. Esposito (2005) classifies videogames as *"a game, which we play, thanks to an audio-visual apparatus and which can be based on a story"*. His definition goes along with Tavinor (2008), who describes videogames as "an artefact in a digital visual medium, which is intented primarily as an object of entertainment, and is intended to provide such entertainment through the employment of one or both of the following modes of engeagement: rule-bound gameplay or interactive fiction". Here, Ikonen (2012) is using the terms Ludologists and Narratology, which in the end signify the same purposes within a game, namely entertainment or a story. Combining these two concepts one must keep in mind that the purpose of making sound effects and background music for any game is to enhance the experience, demonstrate fun and create an attractive atmosphere. Repetition, redundancy and boredom need to be avoided (Drescher, 2006). Further, the sound design being used in this research project combines the approaches of Bernstein (1997) and Ekman (2005), who classify sounds depending on the purpose they have in-game. According to Ikonen (2012) sound design is essential, as it can provide feedback sounds, immerse the player into the game and thus, increase the emotional connection between both.

Acoustic branding can best be described by Krugmann (2007), who sees it as the integrated planning, guiding, controlling and coordination of market-related acoustic stimuli through a determined usage of the whole identity-based brand management process. As not every aspect of an acoustic identity can be taken into account, this study focuses on the sound logo (audio logo), which has been integrated into the sound design of the videogame. A brand's sound logo can be defined as the audio counter-part to a brand's visual logo (audity, 2011). The results are based on the sound logo as well as videogame of the company MLP.

1.2 Theoretical Framework

Directions of the research are focussing on three models, namely classical conditioning, the elaboration likelihood model and the model of musical fit.

Classical Conditioning has been used by Gorn (1982) for the first time in an advertisement context. He was able to demonstrate through an experiment that pleasant, respectively unpleasant music has an effect on brand preference. However, further studies (Allen & Madden, 1985; Kellaris & Cox, 1989) were unable to repeat the outcome.

Based on classical conditioning Petty et. al (1983) developed a model for persuasion, namely the elaboration likelihood model (ELM). A person can be high- or low-involved in a persuasion process. Being in a state of low-involvement, a person can connect the desired object with acoustic cues (Petty et al., 1983).

Further, the model of musical fit states both ways of persuasion, low and high involvement can be influenced through musical cues. However, the musical cues must be fitting, respectively being directed toward the ad, in order to work adequately (MacInnis & Park, 1991; North et al., 2004; Zander, 2006).

The above mentioned models serve as a basis for the hypotheses.

2. Methods

2.1 Hypotheses

Based on the findings from the literature review the following hypotheses have been created and will be tested:

H1: Branded sound design in videogames does not influence the referral rate of users.

H2: Sound logos cannot be learned and recognized by being implemented in the sound design of videogames.

H3: Sound logos learned in-game do not influence brand recall.

H4: Unlearned sound logos do not influence brand recognition.

H5: Videogames with a non-branded sound design do not have an influence on brand recognition.

H6: Videogames with a branded sound design do not have an influence on brand recognition.

H7: Sound logos learned in-game do not influence brand image.

2.2 Research Design

The study used a mixed method approach, containing quantitative as well as qualitative research in the form of an interview and an online survey. Research was conducted over the particular period of eight weeks, making this project cross-sectional (Saunders et al., 2007).

2.3 Research Data Collection and Analysis

The game used in this survey has been developed for MLP's marketing campaign. The tested versions for this study differed in terms of branding only.

In order to test the influence of sound design in videogames on brand awareness, an online survey has been designed. No pilot study was conducted, as the questionnaire was mainly based on previously used data (Vovici, 2008; North et al., 2004; RMS, 2006). Participants were randomly assigned to one out of four groups, 1 control group and 3 test groups. Resulting in at least 30 participants per group, to receive statistically reliable results (Chang & Huang, 2006). However, group sizes differed in numbers. All respondents were confronted with the same demographic questions. The control group was questioned about brand awareness only. The first test group was further questioned about different corporate sound logos. Both groups did not play the videogame. Only the second and third test group were asked to further play the videogame with a non-branded, respectively branded sound design. The groups were then questioned toward their level of recognition, recall and liking of the specific sound logos.

	Playing videogame with		Sound logo	Brand awareness
	Non-branded sound design	Branded sound design		
Control group				x
Test group 1			x	x
Test group 2	x		x	x
Test group 3		x	x	x

Table 1. Test design

Respondents were gathered by spreading it to different universities within Germany. It can be assumed that the results have not been influenced by this as the initial target groups of the game were students as well. Further, the respondents generally fit into the target group of MLP in terms of age, education and occupation. The survey took place for two weeks of the project and each participant was asked between five and 25 questions, depending on the group, they were assigned to. All data was collected anonymously.

In order to test the hypotheses, two different methods have been used, namely the Chi-Square test as well as Cramer's V. Hereby, the Chi-Square method was used to determine associations between categorical variables. A level of 0.05 was the significant threshold. Further, Cramer's V was used to specify the strength between two variables (Saunders et al., 2007).

3. Results

3.1 Descriptive

In total 149 respondents replied to the online survey, of which 61.7% were male and 38.3% female. Further, 71.8% of all respondents were between 22 and 34 years, followed by 19.5 being 21 and younger. Moreover, the majority, with 53% either held a Bachelor or Master's degree. Finally, 66.4% of all respondents were students, while still 24.2% were regular employees.

Besides the regular demographic profile, the survey provided data about the liking of MLP's sound logo. One can see that the participants rated it rather well, if they have played the branded videogame (shift from 46.7% to 66.7%), instead of non-branded (shift from 36.7% to 15.4%).

Moreover, the brand awareness, for the company MLP has been measured. Here, one can see that the control group, which has been exposed to the brand name only, showed a general brand awareness rate of 16%.

3.2 Results

In total seven hypotheses were tested. Whereas the hypotheses had to be accepted in four cases.

The first hypothesis stated that branded sound design in videogames does not influence users referral rate. It had to be accepted, as a Chi-Square score of 0.535 with a degree of freedom of 1 was not significant. Meaning integrating branded sound design has no negative effect on the user experience.

The second hypothesis has proven that integrating sound logos in videogames does not support recognition of the sound logo significantly, as the Chi-Square score of 0.732 shows.

With a Chi-Square score of 10.360 and a degree of freedom of 2 (leading to a p-value of 0.006), a significant correlation between the group variable and the recognition, respectively relation of sound logo to brand, could be measured. The third hypothesis had to be rejected, meaning sound logos learned in videogames aid brand recall. Furthermore, Cramer's V showed a medium-strengthened correlation between the two variables, with a value of 0.323.

As expected, the fourth hypothesis, pointing out that no correlation exists between unlearned sound logos and the level of brand awareness, had to be accepted based on a Chi-Square result of 0.006.

Also the fifth hypothesis which stated that videogames with a non-branded sound design do not have an influence on the level of brand awareness, had to be accepted as it is supported by a Chi-Square result of 0.662 for a degree of freedom of 1.

In addition to the sole recognition of the sound logo, it has been tested whether the branded sound design significantly influences the brand awareness. As mentioned earlier, the brand awareness was at a rate of 16%, which increased to 23.3% for participants that played the non-branded videogame and even to 33.3% after participants played the branded videogame. Despite this strong trend, hypothesis 6 had to be accepted, as a Chi-Square score of 3.651 and a degree of freedom of 1 (leading to a p-value of 0.056) shows.

Also the seventh hypothesis (videogames with a branded sound design cannot influence image values of a brand) had to be accepted. In this example three values show a strong trend by the branded sound design, namely being conservative, trustworthy and conventional. However, the Chi-Square scores were 2.265, 3.651 and 2.735, all of them at a degree of freedom of 1 leading to p-values of 0.132, 0.098 and 0.098.

4. Discussion

4.1 Conclusion

Companies have nothing to lose when integrating branded audio elements into online videogames. As hypotheses 1 proved, it does not make games less attractive for users and demonstrates similar fun as referrals rates have not been influenced. However, companies can use branded audio elements in videogames to enhance their level of brand awareness (strong trend on p=0.0056 level but no significance). Results of the online survey show that participants were able to relate the sound logo significantly more often to a specific brand, after having played the branded videogame. Moreover, brands can influence their level of recognition, by using branded sound designs in their videogames. Finally, brands should consider their desired brand identity and perceived brand image. Previous findings show that music can prime attitudes toward a brand (MacInnis & Park, 1991) as well as connect a brand, which is connected to musical cues to different values (Stewart & Punj, 1988; Stewart et al., 1990). Even though none of the image values has been influenced significantly, it can be concluded that there is a robust trend that videogames have an influence on the brand image. Therefore, future research should take the gap between actual and desired brand image into account.

4.2 Limitations

The findings of the project were as expected; however, there were limitations which should be taken into account for future research.

First, an existing videogame with an existing sound design has been used. Hence, only the factor "branding" has been tested but not the influence of sound design itself. Moreover, the report misses an in-depth analysis of MLP and has been tested for a given set of values, which have not been compared to MLP's desired ones. Thus, different values might be affected as well and influence MLP's brand image. Furthermore, the effect of the game itself has not been tested.

Second, normally users play videogames more often. It might be expected that recognition and recall values will improve with higher contact rates.

Third, the sample sizes required for the Chi-Square to work appropriately is 5, per crosstab calculation. However, as the brand MLP was relatively unknown, an unsufficient number of answers was given. Hence, the answers regarding influence on brand values can be seen as an indicator rather than a statistically significant outcome. Further research should take the demographic as well as psychographic factors into account. In addition, it can be recommended to test the influence on user behaviour, in terms of time played, in order to test the effect of branded sound design on consumers.

References

Allen, C. T., & Madden, T. J. (1985). A Closer Look at Classical Conditioning. The Journal of Consumer Research, 3: pp. 301-315.

audity, (2011). Audio-Branding. [Online] Available at: http://audio-branding.de/ [Accessed 29 April 2012].

Chang, H.-J., & Huang, K.-C. (2006). Determination of Sample Size in Using Central Limit. Theorem for Weibull Distribution. Information and Management Sciences, 17: pp. 31-46.

Djaouti, D. et al. (2008). A Gameplay Definition through Videogame Classification. International Journal of Computer Games Technology, 15 February: p. 7.

Drescher, P. (2006). O'Reilly Digital Media. [Online] Available at: http://digitalmedia.oreilly.com/pub/a/oreilly/digitalmedia/2006/04/26/could-mobile-game-audio-be-more-annoying.html?page=1 [Accessed 27 April 2012].

Esposito, N. (2005). A Short and Simple Definition of What a Videogame is. Compiègne Cedex: Authors & Digital Games Research Association DiGRA.

Gorn, G. J. (1982). The Effects of Music In Advertising On Choice Behavior: A Classical Conditioning Approach. Journal of Marketing, 46: pp. 94-101.

Ikonen, A. (2012). Sound Design in Videogames: Characteristics and Purpose. Personal Interview. [25 April 2012].

Kellaris, J. J., & Cox, A. D. (1989). The Effects of Background Music in Advertising: A Reassessment. Journal of Consumer Research, 16: pp. 113-18.

MacInnis, D. J., & Park, C. W. (1991). The Differential Role of Characteristics of Music on High- and Low-Involvement Consumers'. Processing of Ads. Journal of Consumer Research, 18: pp. 161-173.

North, A. C., Law, R. M., & MacKenzie, L. C. (2004). The Effects of Musical and Voice "Fits" on Responses to Advertisements. Journal of Applied Social Psychology, 34: pp. 1675-1708.

Petty, R. E., Cacioppo, J. T., & Schuhmann, D. (1983). Central and Peripheral Routes to Advertising Effectiveness: The Moderating Role of Involvement. Journal of Customer Research, 10: pp. 135-146.

Rentfrow, P. J., & Gosling, S. D. (2003). The Do Re Mi's of Everyday Life: The Structure and Personality Correlates of Musical Preference. Journal of Personality and Social Psychology, 6(84), pp. 1236-1256.

RMS, (2006). RMS.de. [Online] Available at: http://www.rms.de/fileadmin/pdf/ Publikationen/Markt-_und_Mediaforschung/SoundLogo_Check_9.pdf [Accessed 29 April 2012].

Saunders, M., Lewis, P., & Thornhill, A. (2007). Research Methods for Business Students. 4. ed. Essex: Pearson Educated Limited.

Stewart, D., Farmer, K., & Stannard, C. (1990). Music As a Recognition Cue in Advertising-Tracking Studies. Journal of Advertising Research, August, pp. 39-48.

Stewart, D., & Punj, G. (1988). Effects of Using a Nonverbal (Musical) Cue on Recall and Playback of Television Advertising: Implications for Advertising Tracking. Journal of Business Research, Issue 42, pp. 39-51.

Tavinor, G. (2008). Definition of videogames, Canterbury, New Zealand: Lincoln University.

Vo, Q.-H. (1994). Sound-Engineering. 1. ed. s.l.: Expert Verlag.

Vovici, (2008). Vovici Blog. [Online] Available at: http://blog.vovici.com/blog/ bid/17904/Age-Demographics-in-Survey-Research [Accessed 24 May 2012].

Zander, M. F. (2006). Musical influences in advertising: how music modifies first impressions of product endorsers and brands. Psychology of Music, 4(34), pp. 465-480.

Brand Sounder: A Tool for the Design and Evaluation of Sound Logos and Other Brand Sound Elements

John Groves
GROVES Sound Branding GmbH

Anna-Maria Bartsch
Martin-Luther-University Halle-Wittenberg

Introduction

Although the marketing community has long since been aware of the advantages of "brand" contra "campaign" based sound communications, the choice of sound and music for use in a branding context is often based purely on personal preference. This fact alone is largely responsible for the failure of such sounds to measurably fulfil any basic branding prerequisites. The tool "Brand Sounder" has been developed specifically to address this problem by providing a reliable method for the design and judgement of Brand Sound Elements.

The tool is currently in the prototype stage and is an elaboration of the current GROVES Sound Logo Design and Judgment System. It considers a number of criteria, including: the perceived fit of sound to brand, exclusivity, attention potential, distinctive features, stop criteria and (for operative elements) the usage. The individual qualities of the Brand Sound Element are judged and rated numerically, making them classifiable and comparable. This provides a common perspective of the qualities of the sounds and their suitability as Brand Sound Elements. The tool provides and maintains focus by supplying objective judgement criteria on which better decisions and more informed choices may be made. Especially when more people are involved, using such a method makes it quicker and easier to reach a consensus.

1. Overview

Brand Sounder defines a process for examining the suitability of sounds used, or intended for use in a Sound Branding context. It specifies the necessary properties and defines the specific judgement criteria for evaluating the appropriateness of individual Sound Branding Elements. The tool examines and quantifies the following areas: 1) brand fit, 2) ownability, 3) attention potential, 4) distinctive features and 6) usage (for existing operational brand sounds). The stop criteria (5) can disqualify sounds which are considered to be potentially damaging (**Figure 1**).

The associative and emotional brand fit (M1) examines the suitability of the sound to generate the necessary brand associations and to adequately communicate the brand attributes and emotions. A high level of protectability (M2) is desirable to retain maximum individuality and to protect against usage that may create negative associations. The ability of a sound to gain the consumer's attention is analysed in step 3 (M3). Further parameters are the basic GROVES Sound Branding criteria: "concise", "distinct", "memorable" and "flexible" (M4). "Special stop criteria" (stop-module M5) considers parameters that could make a sound unsuitable for use in a branding context, for instance: lack of individuality, contrary brand associations and other such factors. The final module is concerned with implementation and examines the homogeneity and consistency of use of the Brand Sounds (M6).

2. Elaboration of the Individual Modules

2.1 The associative Brand Fit (M1 Submodule 1)

The first module (M1.1.1) examines the ability of a sound to communicate specific brand attributes and to trigger defined associations. The tool assumes that specific sounds, music genre and forms of instrumentation can be measurably linked to specific knowledge or memories.

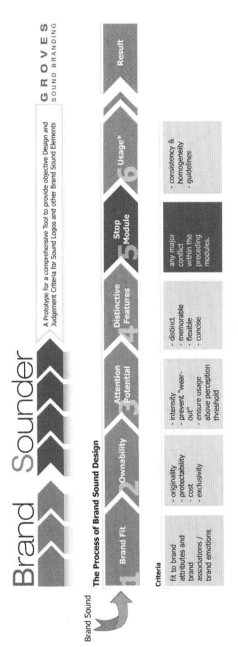

Figure 1. The Process of Brand Sound Design
(*"Usage" module only for implemented Sound Elements)

The suitability is primarily judged with information gained via an internal workshop, a focus group or similar testing methods. These learnings are combined with expert analyse and judgement as well as reference to a continuously growing bank of linked sound/association data. The sub-module M1.1.2 deals with the non-brand specific associations. The module "audio-vision" (M1.1.3) addresses "synchrese" and the specific relationship of sound to shape, form and words. (the "Bouba/Kiki" theory). "Synchrese" (cf. Chion, 1994, 2007, 2009; cf. Murch, 1994) also describes the fusion of moving picture and sound.

Basis: Although the perception of music is widely considered to be subjective, our research shows that a common understanding level of +70% can be reached. Regrading M1.1.3: As auditory stimuli are perceived and processed faster than visual signals, the result is that the hearable part of such an amalgam generates an added value for interpretation. Auditive cues are not only capable of enforcing visual messages but also changing the perception of them. For instance, a moving picture with surf accompanied by the sound of thunder, will inevitably evoke another impression than the sound of seagulls and the peaceful burbling of water. "Kiki" and "Bouba" also refer to synaesthetic perceptions (cf. Groves, 2011, p. 21 f.). Sharp high-pitched sounds will often be associated with "Kiki", whereas a round, whole, low-pitched chord progression will largely be perceived as being connected to "Bouba". The neuronal connections which are created, respectively served, through multi-sensual nexuses, are responsible for the long-term memory of brands (cf. Walewski, 2001, p. 41; cf. Fahlenbrach, 2008, pp. 221 f.).

The final section of this module forms the semantic sound analysis and interpretation (M1.1.4). "Sound objects" can be circumscribed from each other by duration, timbre, frequency and volume (cf. Schafer, 1971, p. 55; Chion, 2009 [1983]; Flückiger, 2006). Sound objects are semantically based on cultural-social traditions, conventions and evolutionary knowledge. The functions of these "Sonic Sememes" are thoroughly examined and interpreted.

2.2 The emotional Brand Fit (M1 Submodule 2)

Having examined links to specific associations, the tool will now establish if the brand has any over-arching emotions that could or should be communicated in general. Either there is a specifically defined brand emotion (e. g. "Joy of Driving") or another specific emotion is dominant (M1.2.1). The next step is the music psychological brand sound analysis (cf. Kreutz, 2008, p. 560; cf. Juslin, 2001, p. 315). The sound is examined to identify and assess the emotions that it is capable of triggering (if any) and whether these emotions fit or contradict the brand's core attributes (**Table 1**). In addition, the level of power of the auditory emotional impression is assessed (M1.2.2).

	Parameter	examples for parameter
A	Key	minor/major
B	Dynamics	forte, piano
C	Articulation	legato/staccato
D	Timbre	bright, dark, round

Table 1. Music psychological parameters of emotional brand fit

The sounds are then examined according to the theory of audiovisual metaphors by Fahlenbrach (2007, 2008). Occurrence and power of the aroused emotions are interpreted (M1.2.3). They are also considered regarding their "auditory mapping". Those which convey auditory images, for instance Audi's "heartbeat", are inspected to establish if adequate specific brand emotions are evoked. (Kövecses, 2007, 2000, 1990; Forceville, 2009; Bartsch/Hübner 2004).

2.3 Ownability (M2)

Whereas it is advisable from the outset to create and use original proprietary sounds, some brands nonetheless invest millions in building up an association to properties that are neither ownable nor protectable. Also, when expanding into new territories, some may discover that their particular sound (usually a song) is already associated with another product or is occupied in another way. This is the reason that a Sound Identity development process must include an adequate Market Review, although this may not always help brands that are using commercially available music in their communications. For instance, in the 60's, a holiday company used the song "Singing in the Rain" for a TV campaign, while at exactly the same time the song was being used in the film "Clockwork Orange" as background for scenes of people getting kicked and abused. This provides the potential for the music to be associated with violence, creating the possibility of it negatively influencing perception of the brand.

The module [M2] will seek to answer the following questions: Is the sound original and new or is it generic? Can the sound be legally protected? (e.g. It is not possible to protect everyday sounds.) Is a licence for unlimited exclusive use affordable – or even possible? Does the sound/ music contain any freely available or protected sound-samples?

2.4 Attention Potential (M3)

Sounds that are used seldom or in situations where gaining attention is important or even mandatory – such as alarms and warnings – must have a high attention potential. On the other hand, very strident sounds which are used in high exposure situations – such as TV advertising – may be in danger of damaging perception by causing irritation. By identifying this potential, it may be possible to introduce parameters and measures that will guard against this, i.e. reducing the potentially damaging element (sound parameter) or prescribing variation. To do this, the ability of a sound to get attention is examined and quantified. It is possible to quantify and measure a sound's intensity by observing certain specific parameter such as: volume, tempo, dynamics (e.g. playing technique), general sound impression and then identifying the potentially negative parameter. These could take the form of excessive low/high frequencies, high levels of compression, special or strange timbres, unusual intervals/chords and so on.

A projection or estimation of the frequency of use and exposure may help to prevent "wear-out" or respectively ensure optimal usage above the perception threshold.

2.5 Distinctive Features (M4)

This module examines a number of properties of the element, such as its level of "differentiation" from the existing Sound Elements of competitors and others, (optimally based on the findings of a Market Review), "memorability" – the quality for recall, "conciseness" – the amount of time the element needs to be recognised and create an association to the brand and "flexibility" – the potential for adaption for use in further Sound Elements.

2.6 Stop Module (M5)

The end results of the examination of the individual criteria are weighted in order of importance providing an end score. Although the Sound Brander provides useful comparative valuations and indicates that a high score equals high suitability, a high overall score is also possible when a Sound Element has been judged to be optimal in most categories but very low or zero in just one. The purpose of the stop module is to identify such phenomena and prohibit the consideration of elements that have any danger for causing a negative effect. Therefore, when the stop module is triggered, it will effectively disqualify any elements which could be potentially damaging, regardless of their overall score.

2.7 Usage (M6)

Cross-media monitoring is conducted to measure consistency of use, which is a key success factor for all forms of branding. Using unrelated Sound Elements in the individual applications will severely impair brand recognisability and diminish the chances of triggering the desired association with the brand via the sense of hearing. The actual usage of the Brand Sound will be carefully monitored, with attention being paid to the quality of adaption in the individual applications/touch-points (conceptual), the general quality perception (technical), homogeneity of tual), the general quality perception (technical), homogeneity of sound with picture and clearness (e.g. intelligibility when used together with a speaker).

General: Rules should be defined and agreed upon to prescribe which Branding Element will be used where, when and how. This is best done by the implementation of a Brand Sound Guide. These days, such guides are often incorporated into a website, where all brand information, including an archive of the actual Brand Elements, are stored and made available. Users and potential users should be involved as early as possible. They should be given all information necessary to gain their support in creating a common understanding of the Sound Branding process (Stakeholder Buy-in). Subsequently, steps must be taken to ensure compliance.

3. The Implementation and the Future of the Brand Sounder

The necessity for sound evaluation is an important topic for those responsible in brand communications. Establishing such a common method will require the acceptance and support of all those who have an influence on how brands are perceived. Brand Sounder aims to provide universal process guidelines and common objective criteria for the design and judgement of brand sounds. Its use will contribute to better and more efficient sound communication by ensuring that relevant, clear and consistent brand messages are sent in all channels.

References

Bartsch, Anne/Jens Eder/Kathrin Fahlenbrach (Eds.) (2007). Audiovisuelle Emotionen. Emotionsdarstellung und Emotionsvermittlung durch audiovisuelle Medienangebote. Köln: Herbert-von-Halem-Verlag.

Bartsch, Anne/Susanne Hübner (2004). Emotionale Kommunikation – ein integratives Modell. Dissertation. Halle (Saale): Universität Halle.

Bruhn, Herbert/Reinhard Kopiez/Andreas C. Lehmann (Eds.) (2008). Musikpsychologie. Das neue Handbuch. Reinbek bei Hamburg: Rowohlt.

Chion, Michel (2009). Film: a Sound Art. New York: Columbia University Press.

Chion, Michel (2007). Audio-Vision and Sound. In: Kruth, Patricia/Henry Stobart (eds.), Sound. pp. 201-221. Cambridge: Cambridge University Press.

Chion, Michel (1994). Audio-vision: sound on screen. Ed. and transl. by Claudia Gorbman. New York: Columbia University Press.

Fahlenbrach, Kathrin (2008). Habilitationsschrift: Audiovisuelle Metaphern. Zur Körper- und Affektästhetik in Film und Fernsehen. Halle (Saale): Universität Halle.

Fahlenbrach, Kathrin (2007). Audiovisuelle Metaphern und Emotionen im Sound-Design. In: Bartsch, Anne/Jens Eder/Kathrin Fahlenbrach (eds.). Audiovisuelle Emotionen. Emotionsdarstellung und Emotionsvermittlung durch audiovisuelle Medien. pp. 330-349. Köln: Herbert-von-Halem-Verlag.

Flückiger, Barbara (2002). Sound Design. Die virtuelle Klangwelt des Films. Marburg: Schüren.

Forceville, Charles J./Eduardo Urios-Aparasi (eds.) (2009). Multimodal Metaphor. Berlin/New York: Mouton de Gruyter.

Forceville, Charles J. (2009). The role of non-verbal sound and music in multimodal metaphor. In: Forceville, Charles J. & Eduardo Urios-Aparasi (eds.). Multimodal Metaphor. pp. 383-40. Berlin/New York: Mouton de Gruyter.

Groves, John (2011). ComMUSICation. From Pavlov's Dog to Sound Branding. Cork, Ireland: Oak Tree Press.

Juslin, Patrik N./ John A. Sloboda (eds.) (2001). Music and Emotion: Theory and Research. Oxford: Oxford University Press.

Juslin, Patrik N. (2001). Communicating emotion in music performance: a review and a theoretical framework. In: Juslin, Patrik N. / John A. Sloboda (eds.). Music and Emotion: Theory and Research. pp. 309-337. Oxford: Oxford University Press.

Kövecses, Zoltán (2007). Metaphor in Culture: universality and variation. Cambridge: Cambridge University Press.

Kövecses, Zoltán (2000). Metaphor and Emotion. Language, Culture, and Body in Human Feeling. Cambridge: Cambridge University Press.

Kövecses, Zoltán (1990). Emotion Concepts. New York / Berlin / Heidelberg: Springer-Verlag.

Kreutz, Gunter (2008). Musik und Emotion. In: Bruhn, Herbert/Reinhard Kopiez/Andreas C. Lehmann (eds.). Musikpsychologie. Das neue Handbuch, pp. 548-572. Reinbek bei Hamburg: Rowohlt.

Murch, Walter (1994). Foreword. In: Chion, Michel. Audio-vision. Sound on Screen. pp. 7-24. New York: Columbia University Press.

Schafer, Raymond Murray (1971). Die Schallwelt in der wir leben. Wien: Universal Edition.

Walewski, Michael (2001). Musik in der Fernsehwerbung. Eine empirische Untersuchung des durch TV-Werbemusik ausgelösten Wirkungsprozesses (Inaugural-Dissertation für Doktorgrad). Münster: Universität Münster.

Sounding Façades

Abel Korinsky, Carlo Korinsky, Max Korinsky, Clarissa Khan

Korinsky – Atelier für vertikale Flächen

Key Words

vertical sound, multisensual branding in open space, sounding façades, acoustic illusions, acoustic perception

Abstract

Façades get a voice – The distribution of sound on façades requires a new approach to human hearing, as human perception is predominantly conditioned on horizontal sound. Through *Sounding Façades*, buildings of companies and institutions become sensory landmarks. They become part of the urban sound scenery. *Sounding Façades* draw attention and appeal to the passersby as well as the customer or employees inside the building.

A *Sounding Façade* could (not only) be the façade of a building, but also any other vertical plane installed with an organised system of loudspeakers that plays site-specific soundscapes, that could also be used to communicate the owners' brand identity. Using the *Vertical Sound Lab Software*, it is posssible to create realistic and illusionary sensory experiences, connecting the building or structure, its function, surroundings and the passersby. Through the experience of soundscapes people are drawn to the building by a sensational atmosphere based on sound.

The outside appearance reflects the inside, and vice versa. A conditioning of the brand identity takes place. The *Sounding Façade* offers new communication opportunities through an audio instrument, which communicates a multisensory brand identity. Furthermore, tonal façades set new standards in human acoustic perception. It is important to recognise the acoustic potential of façades and to form a tonal correlation to developments in lighting design.

1. Sound Branding and Sound Staging in Open Space

In today's multimedia society more than 700,000 brands (in Germany) bid for the favour of customers (Sattler & Völckner, 2007). Due to increasing product homogeneity and the classification in high-class and functional, differences are being less and less recognizable. To stand out and survive among the mass of brands that exist today, it becomes more important to stimulate various senses simultaneously in order to communicate a message multi-sensually. Consequently, it is necessary to provide a clear and comprehensive brand experience.

Figure 1. Sounding façade – Max-Schmeling-Halle, Berlin

One relatively new but growing discipline of multi-sensual branding is *Sound Branding*, which deals with the sound of brands / tonal identity of a brand – starting from product sounds and sound logos to entire brand songs.

Abel Korinsky, Carlo Korinsky, Max Korinsky, Clarissa Khan

Nowadays, it is necessary to extend the present term of *sound branding* from an audio form of brand communication to include the dimension of space. Adding the concept of Sounding Façades – and accordingly the factor "space" – to common Sound Branding portfolios could be the beginning of a new era. The presentation of a brand through the tonal staging of façades in public space results in a natural affiliation between the brand and the building, for example shops, offices, museums and places of interest or any visible façade of what a brand represents. It is an insightful, conceptual and technical achievement.

Advertising mostly works with a direct and easily understood message that is quickly communicated to a large audience. Compared to the usual advertisement, the sounding façade works with a much broader spectrum of possibilities. The success does not measure itself exclusively in sales figures, but rather in the lasting effect on the individual viewer. That is why a Sounding Façade opens up a broad new field – i.e., in its simplicity, unobtrusiveness and inconspicuousness it is still able to attract a lot of attention.

2. The Difference Between Vertical and Horizontal Perception of Sound. A Short Presentation of Qualitative Differences.

Human evolutionary history and the physiological position of our two ears explain a sense of hearing that is far clearer and more differentiated on the horizontal plane than the vertical (Guski, 2006). *"Studies of human localization have demonstrated that vertical localization depends on the same variables as monaural localization in the horizontal plane."* describes Heffner (1992, p. 701). It is mainly due to the ears' position on the sides of our head, that we best perceive sound coming from our right and left. Therefore we use horizontal tonal planes to localise ourselves. Additionally, in former times, humans had few predators that came from above and even for hunting the vertical sense of hearing was not necessary as the important prey lived on the ground.

The general difference between vertical and horizontal tonal perception is in the localization of sounds. Highly developed as our horizontal hearing is, our ability to locate sounds above our head is imprecise: Localization is difficult because sound sources are usually perceived as much broader than on the horizontal plane, along which they can easily be pinpointed. Under favourable conditions, humans can locate a sound on the horizontal plane accurately up to 1 degree – on the vertical plane it is only up to 4 degrees, which was discovered in scientific studies about how humans use auditory perceptions to accurately locate interesting activities (Guski, 2006).

Through using a vertical tonal plane, it is therefore possible to create illusionary effects. When the sounds come from above, we make mistakes and confuse whether the sounds come from in front or behind, and are also unable to distinguish from what distance above us the sound originates. There is furthermore a connection between the tonal frequencies and the height of the space; the higher the frequency, the higher we perceive the source of the sound (Guski, 1989).

Our brain can calculate an exact horizontal position using information of differences in the sound's arrival time to each ear as well as phase differences, amplitude and filtering (Dickreiter, 2008). In contrast sound from above arrives at both ears simultaneously so time and amplitude differences are no longer useful for determining the position. Thus humans localize these sonic events less precisely.

How can these deficiencies in vertical hearing generally be used?

- They can be technically compensated to avoid irritation.
- They can be used to increase irritations or create deceptions and illusions. In this way the listener experiences new perceptual phenomena and events.

3. How to Use and Control the Deficiencies of Human Audition on the Vertical Plane: The Vertical Sound Lab Software as a Tool.

'Korinsky – Atelier für vertikale Flächen' has developed an innovative software (Vertical Sound Lab) that enables the conceptual and technical application of Sound Branding and Sound Design on façades. The software is based on scientific research about human hearing and uses the special characteristics of vertical sound perception to create effects and experiences, e.g. acoustic illusions. This new perceptual phenomenon is comparable to the visual 3D-effect – although this is already known about, it provides a pleasing experience time and time again.

As a tool for the creation of *Sounding Façades* Korinsky's Vertical Sound Lab software allows a meticulous sound distribution on different loudspeakers affixed to a façade. The software processes the given data of the façade and loudspeakers positions to allow different kinds of sound reproduction over the loudspeakers.

The calculation of transit-time differences (i.e. the speed of the sound from one loudspeaker to the hearing position on the ground), is one of its basic functions. A Doppler effect can be simulated (natural phenomenon of moving sound sources) and reverb, filters and different volumes and pitches between the different loudspeakers are automatically controlled.

These main effects are generated by the software in order to create a new three-dimensional sensation of hearing and to simulate movement of sounds in a certain area. That means sounds do not come only from one speaker, rather they seem to be free to move around and change position within a room even though the speaker does not physically change its position.

The software enables rotating, permanently oscillating and changing (kinds of) sounds. Distribution of soundscapes and figures, chance functions, the possibility to use any number of speakers and the impression of three dimensional hearing on a two dimensional wall are special features. Using certain kinds of speakers a sounding depth can be generated while directed speakers can create a feeling of closeness (comparable to the impression of hearing while using headphones).

4. Perceptual Phenomena

In the future companies will show new forms of acoustic perception in form of *Sounding Façades*. It is only sound specialists who know the existence of this acoustic potential at the moment.

Such psychophysical effects (Hall, 2008) on *Sounding Façades* can show following perceptual phenomena (a selection of effects):

- Perception of the whole wall as one big loudspeaker.
- Altered perception of the distance of the sound (sensation of a very close earphone versus distant).
- A perception of moving sound sources on the vertical façade.
- An illusion of endless rising or lowering tone pitches as in Deutsch's scale illusion (comparable to the visual *M.C. Escher´s* "Relativity" with the perception of an endlessly rising staircase).

To make it clearer to non-sound-researchers it is easier to compare this technique with the effect of 3D-cinema: An already known human sense can be exposed to absolutely new, and not previously known, forms of understanding.

Sounding Façades could result in a new approach to the visual appearance. The combination of different illusions would allow an apparently fluctuating display of a Sounding Façade and is able to change its perception, e.g., of a building by creating a tonal atmosphere. Thanks to of the novelty of the technique, it will appeal to the curiosity of the individual, as well as create a more intensive experience. Companies have to use these new ways of multi-sensual branding to create unique and engaging experiences that will be related to their brand.

5. Sound Staging on Façades

For a very long time the corporate identity has been represented mainly through visual design. Companies and institutions with fixed locations should use their façades to provide an experience of the brand on an audio and spatial level. A sound in open space or on façades will create attention, recognition, differentiation and also the mediation of information as well as associations, which communicate and emotionalise the brand identity on a new dimension.

Multi-sensual marketing of brands increases an experience for consumers, and by connection of the visual façade with an advertisement, decoration, lighting etc. – the optical and acoustic stimuli compliment and enhance each other.

Due to the exclusivity and innovation of staging the brands, the buildings themselves become a form of *location anchoring*, and communicate the brand on the façade. Whether a flagship store, headquarters or salesroom – the tonal staging of façades is applicable in various ways.

The process of sounding façades contains following steps:

- The examination of the brand and site-specific characteristics of a place, which influence the production of the sound design.
- Analysis of site-specific main frequencies.
- The investigation of a tonality, which connects brand and environment with each other.
- Formulation of the concept.
- Finally: the installation of the acoustic façade.

6. Fundamental Focuses in Staging Sounding Façades

6.1 Analytical and technical implementation

The reflective behaviour of façades and the available spectrum of sounds of the surroundings have to be analysed and used as influencing factors in staging the *Sounding Façade*. An acoustic intervention in the natural sphere of sound creates an additional benefit for the brand and for the locality.

6.2 Acoustic brand design of façades

The existing brand identity of the company could be taken as the basis. Then it is necessary to ascertain the brand values that are to be communicated, which will be converted into a tonality. These brand values are compiled into an acoustic branding, which becomes the final audible façade. In addition to online-marketing-strategies, companies are increasingly investing in displaying products in their company offices and sales rooms. The purchasing of something physical is a shopping experience where the customer is drawn into the shop by such things as events, actions, and interactive advertisement. Sounding Façades should aim to present the brand as a sensational experience for the costumer.

People are still interested in encountering a brand through a unique and physical experience. A proof of this is the number of Flagship-Stores that offer an event of some kind or design character. Companies, institutions and venues have to create emotions, feelings, and attention, as well as rouse curiosity in the customer to sell a product affiliated with a lifestyle. The use of different media production and design of sales rooms and façades is essential to communicate the attitude and lifestyle of a brand, and furthermore, to translate these emotions on to the product. The shopping experience expected in cities is one of sensation and atmosphere through the attentive curation of the sales room and its products.

Figure 2. Sounding façade ("Z9") – Humboldt University, Berlin

Today's façades are elaborately designed visually (using lights, screens, plantations, mega posters, etc.), but there is no similar development of vertical surfaces using sound. The visual design of a façade is not enough to distinguish a company clearly from its competition. *Sounding Façades* have the enormous advantage that they immediately stimulate our perception and emotions, both consciously and subconsciously. Now the only competition is with the tonal environment.

Subsequently, it is necessary to distinguish the *Sounding Façade* clearly from its acoustic surroundings by using an individual frequency spectrum.

7. Interactivity and Modification

Furthermore it is necessary for companies and shops to use different sensors, video tracking, and motion triggers to create a 'playground' for the customer.

For example, light-, temperature-, movement-, detection-, gravity-, and motion-sensors can be used to control the parameters of sound. In the future it will more and more interesting with the connection of *Sounding Façades* with social networks like Twitter and Facebook, creating a more diverse and interactive possibilities where tweets or facebook statuses will be able to influence the soundscape.

7.1 Integration of surroundings

Locations and façades have to be analysed to integrate sounds in the urban soundscape. Factors such as the frequency spectrum, material of the façade, and sound reflection are calculated to install a façade with an individual sound design. Sound should not be an annoying medium, but become part of the urban soundscape to enrich the surroundings.

7.2 Avoidance of disturbing noise or sound

Sound emissions can be reduced very easy when using special focused audio spotlights (similar to LED-spotlights). It is also important to analyse the area to find out the sound reflection. Consequently, the desired effect will not be affected by restraint and inconspicuousness of the application of sound.

7.3 Change

Futhermore, the use of general acoustics in the application of a Sounding Façade is not a static one and sound branding brings a new dimension. In difference to 'normal' sound branding the sound in the open space can change over a longer period of time. This avoids constantly recurring structures, creates high recognition and results in a consistent audio atmosphere.

References

Dickreiter, M. (2008). Handbuch der Tonstudiotechnik. Band 1. München: K. G. Saur Verlag.

Guski, R. (2006). Wahrnehmung – ein Lehrbuch, (http://eco.psy.ruhr-uni-bochum.de/ecopsy/download/Guski-Lehrbuch/Kap_7_2.html), accessed December 16, 2012. Stuttgart: Kohlhammer.

Guski, R. (1989). Wahrnehmung, p. 129. Stuttgart: Kohlhammer.

Hall, D. E. (2008). Musikalische Akustik. Ein Handbuch, pp. 104-105. Mainz: Schott Music.

Heffner, R. S. & Heffner, H. E. (1992). Evolution of sound in localization in mammals. In D. B. Webster, R. R. Fay, and A. N. Popper (Eds.), The Evolutionary Biology of Hearing, pp. 691-715. New-York: Springer-Verlag.

Sattler, H, Völckner, F. (2007). Markenpolitik. Stuttgart: Kohlhammer.

About the Authors

Susan Aminoff
Susan has spent her career at the forefront of emerging branding and marketing practices, helping clients leverage innovative tools for brand impact and advantage. As Managing Director of Elias Arts Audio Branding Division, Susan helps brands strategically leverage the use of music and sound for deeper emotional engagement with their consumers, partners and employees; to create greater marketplace distinction; and to help brands create coherency across touchpoints – yielding bottom line results. Elias Arts is credited with pioneering the discipline of Audio Branding back in 1980, and has been setting the standards in the industry ever since. Susan has personally led engagements for American Express, Bloomberg, Citi, Cisco, Comcast, Dell, Travelers and Verizon, among others.

Michele Arnese
Michele Arnese, designed in Italy and assembled in Germany, is co-founder and co-owner of amp – audible brand and corporate communication. He has a degree in Engineering at University of Pisa and worked more than 10 years as management consultant for major German and international companies. His passion for music could take advantage from the experience of methods, strategy and ideas: he is the head of strategy and consultancy at amp.

Anna-Maria Bartsch

Anna-Maria completed her studies of media and communication science, English and American studies as well as German literature at the Martin-Luther-University Halle-Wittenberg. With a focus "Sound Branding", she wrote her final thesis on "Cinematic Effects in the Sound Branding of TV spots". The idea for a tool to evaluate and design Brand Sound was derived from this work. Together with John Groves and Christoph Groß-Fengels from GROVES Sound Communications, she developed the concept for "Brand Sounder", a tool based on the existing GROVES method. It was first presented at the Audio Branding Congress, which took place at Oxford University in December 2012.

Kai Bronner

Kai Bronner studied media economics and graduated (graduate engineer) with a diploma thesis about audio branding in 2004. Since then, Kai gained experience in the field of audio branding, sound communication, sound design and has been supervising research projects on sound and crossmodal effects. In 2007 and 2009, he became the editor and author of two compilation books about audio branding. In 2009, Kai founded with his fellows Cornelius Ringe and Rainer Hirt the Audio Branding Academy in Hamburg. In addition to his general interest in music, his main research interests include sound communication, sound design, sound & multisensory connections.

Juan Corrales

Licenced in Business administration and master in ebusiness, Juan worked in peermusic (4th global music publisher) as General Manager for Latin American Operations and European Film & TV Director before moving in 2001 to the Advertising and Digital world where he stayed for 10 years in BBDO working for top international and local brands and receiving multiple awards such as Cannes Gold Lions or DMA Diamond & Gold Echo among many others. He was Managing Director for development and Digital in Contrapunto BBDO and member of the board when he left the company in 2011 to found Flyabit. For the last 10 years he has developed business devoted to using sound and music as a communication tool in areas such as retail music systems, live music, advertising, film & TV, digital and Sound Branding. In 2012, he founded Flyabit Sound & Digital studio.

Henry Daw

Henry Daw works as a Principal Sound Designer for Nokia, based at the Nokia Design Studio in central London. Henry's musical background started out very early with the classical piano, which later on progressed to creative music technology. This culminated in a Music Degree at RWCMD in Cardiff with a Principal Study in Music Technology. After graduating in 2002, Henry relocated to Tampere Finland where he would form part of the new Nokia Sound Design Team. Henry has since overseen the development of Nokia sound for over 10 years. Over the years Henry's role at Nokia has seen him responsible for the sounds of Nokia's Nseries flagship range, working alongside various artists such as Brian Eno and Kruder & Dorfmeister on the Premium range of handsets, developing the extensive regional ringtone offering, and overseeing the most recent core brand sounds renewal work which included the refreshed Nokia tune.

Dr. Hauke Egermann
In 2006 he completed a Magister Artium program at the Hanover University of Music, Drama and Media in Systematic Musicology, Media Science and Applied Communication Research. Subsequently he graduated in the PhD program at the Hanover Center of Systemic Neurosciences. From 2009 to 2011 he joined the Centre for Interdisciplinary Research for Music Media and Technology, McGill University as Postdoctoral Research Fellow. Since 2011 he is Research Associate and Lecturer in the Audio Communication Group, Technische Universität Berlin. His research and teaching interests are centered around communication and perception of music and sound. In parallel to his academic work, Hauke Egermann works freelance for different applied research and marketing consulting companies.

Stephanie Forge
Stephanie Forge has a Master Degree in Popular Music and Media and is a Research Assistant and PhD candidate at the Institute for Research on Musical Ability (IBFM) at the University of Paderborn in Germany. Since 2008 she teaches at the University of Paderborn courses such as music in advertising and conducts research on consumer behavior and the effects of sound branding.

Dr. Klaus Frieler

Klaus Frieler received a diploma in Physics and a PhD in Systematic Musicology. Since 2000 he is working as a freelance software developer, music expert witness, and scientific consultant. From 2008 to 2012 he held a position as a lecturer in Systematic Musicology at the University of Hamburg, followed by a three-month research stint at the Centre for Digital Music, Queen Mary College, London. Since autumn 2012 he is working as a post-doc researcher at the Hochschule für Musik Franz Liszt Weimar.

John Groves

In the early 90s John Groves became one of the pioneers of Sound Branding, by developing a structured system for the creation and implementation of brand and corporate Sound Identities. The client list of GROVES Sound Communications contains a number of distinguished brands such as Olympus, Wrigley's, Mentos, Bacardi, Audi, Nivea, BMW, Visa, TUI as well as a large number of radio and TV stations. He is president of the Composers Club, Germany, vice president of FFACE – the Federation of Film and Audio-visual Composers of Europe, board member of ECSA – the European Composers and Songwriters Alliance, and member of the Art Directors Club.

Rainer Hirt

Studies in communication design at the University of Applied Sciences, Konstanz (Master of Arts). While still a communication design student, Rainer founded the corporate sound information portal www.audio-branding.de, which became well known in professional circles. Rainer acts as managing partner of audity, an agency specialised in audio branding with clients such as Danone, Symrise and Volkswagen. Rainer Hirt is also an author and co-producer of the compendium "Audio-Branding" and since 2007, has been supervising various research projects with several universities. Additionally, Hirt has been a juror for the international red dot design award in 2008 and 2009.

Dr. Cristy Ho

Cristy Ho received her DPhil degree in experimental psychology from the University of Oxford, UK. She is currently a postdoctoral research scientist at the Crossmodal Research Laboratory at Oxford. Her research has focused on investigating the effectiveness of multisensory warning signals in driving. She received the American Psychology Association's New Investigator Award in Experimental Psychology: Applied in 2006.

Russell Jones
Russell Jones is co-founder and creative director of Condiment Junkie, a sensory design agency that specialize in experiential sound and scent, sonic branding and sensory strategy. His work is underpinned by scientific research into how senses interact, coupled with innovative creative ideas and a keen attention to the finer details. Condiment Junkie work with premium brands to maximise the use of sound across all communications, specialising in sensory strategy and brand experiences. After initially studying film, Russell began his career writing and producing music under the pseudonym Victor Malloy, and working with dance choreographers exploring movement and sound in film and on stage. He also regularly lectures on the effects of environmental sound on our emotions and perception.

Scott King
Scott King is co-founder and director of Condiment Junkie, a sensory design agency that specialize in experiential sound and scent, sonic branding and sensory strategy. Scott has over 15 years experience masterminding sensory marketing strategies and brand communications for some of the world's most innovative organisations.

Dr. Klemens Knöferle
Coming from a background in musicology, Klemens Knöferle obtained a Ph.D. in Marketing from the University of St. Gallen, Switzerland, and is now a postdoctoral fellow at the Crossmodal Research Laboratory at the Department of Experimental Psychology, Oxford University. His research focuses on how sensory aspects of products and retail environments influence consumers' emotions, perceptions, preferences, and behaviour. Klemens is particularly interested in interactions between different sensory modalities, and builds on current insights from the fields of cognitive psychology and psychophysics into how our various senses process information and interact with each other. Moreover, Klemens specializes in the influence of auditory cues (such as product-inherent sounds and music) on consumer behaviour.

Korinsky – Atelier für vertikale Flächen
Combining competences in art, design and communications, Berlin-based art collective Korinsky – Atelier für vertikale Flächen mainly focuses on sound installations on façades or other vertical surfaces – the higher the better. As they developed a special Sound Art Software, they are able to create unknown audiovisual illusions and new room experiences by using the knowledge about the imprecision of vertical hearing. For their innovative artistic and technological approach the team got awarded with the title Kultur- & Kreativpiloten by the Initiative of Culture- & Creative Economy of the German Government. They furthermore get sponsored with the Exist-Scholarship for Start-Up Entrepreneurs by the German Federal Ministry of Economy & Technology, the European Union.

Evelyn Kreb
Having studied Popular Music and Media at the University of Paderborn (Germany), Evelyn Kreb is conducting her research at the intersection of musicological and sociological subjects. Working in different companies as a translator and interpreter permitted her insights in business structures and communication. Theoretical education, practical experience in recording and music publishing as well as musical practice form the basis for her musical creativity based research on sound branding. Currently, Evelyn Kreb is continuing her studies at the Universities of Paris-Sorbonne (France) and Saarbrücken (Germany) in the Master's program of International Musicology.

Patrick Langeslag
Patrick Langeslag studied business administration at the University of Antwerp and graduated with a major in international economics. In 2001, he founded the audio consulting group together with Wilbert Hirsch. As senior partner strategy, he advises major companies in acoustic branding and corporate identity. Patrick Langeslag serves as an external lecturer for audio branding at several universities. He has been a member of the New York Academy of Science since 2003.

Natalia Lannes

Natalia Lannes is Account Manager at Gomus. Brazil. She completed a Marketing MBA at Fundação Getúlio Vargas RJ, Brazil and holds a B.A. in Business Management & Media Communications at Webster University, Geneva Switzerland.

Rudi Mauser

Rudi Mauser, born in Germany, is co-founder and co-owner of amp – audible brand and corporate communication. He studied music at the Richard Strauss Conservatory in Munich and has been working more than 20 years as musician and composer for numbers of international artists and film & TV productions / theatres / brands. This experience helped him to develop over the years a profound knowledge about the function and the emotional effect of music: he is the head of music and production at amp.

Alex Moulton

Best known as the founder of Expansion Team, Alex recently merged his audio branding firm with Eyeball, the design company-turned ad agency led by long-time collaborator Limore Shur. With Expansion Team, Alex was responsible for crafting the sound of many TV networks including CNN International, PBS and Discovery, and contributed his expertise to respected brands like jetBlue, Amazon and Verizon. An acclaimed recording artist and DJ by night, it was Alex's early years at Eyeball as an editor/director that led him to launch Expansion Team. Seeing a growing need for authentic music in the ad world, he assembled a roster of recording artists, DJs and Grammy-winning songwriters and became a pioneer in the audio branding field. By joining forces with Eyeball once again, he continues his vision for more engaging and effective brand building.

Dr. Daniel Müllensiefen

Daniel Müllensiefen studied Systematic Musicology, Historic Musicology and Journalism at the universities of Hamburg (Germany) and Salamanca (Spain). He did his doctoral dissertation in Systematic Musicology on memory for melodies at the University of Hamburg and obtained his PhD in 2004. From 2006 until 2009 he worked as a Research Fellow in the Computing department at Goldsmiths, University of London. In 2009 he joined the Psychology department at Goldsmiths where he is now a senior lecturer and co-director of the Master's course in Music, Mind and Brain. In 2010 he was also appointed as Scientist in Residence with the London-based advertising agency DDB UK where he acts as a consultant and researcher, mainly on questions regarding the role of music in advertising and other commercial settings.

239

Rayan Parikh
Rayan joined Elias Arts in 2003 to conquer the last frontier of integrated marketing: audio. Deploying his experience in branding, UX and experiential marketing, Rayan formalized the core components of Elias' audio branding methodology, including best practices and audio branding taxonomies, and has helped develop Audio Identity Systems™ for Cisco, Nike, Coca-Cola, Sun Microsystems and Orange Wireless. Rayan has created numerous "Best Practices" modules and authored White Papers and book chapters on the discipline of Audio Branding. Prior to joining Elias Arts, Rayan was Director of Brand Strategy for The Futurebrand Co. in New York. Rayan holds a BA in European History from the University of North Carolina at Chapel Hill, and a MBA from Georgetown University in Washington DC.

Johannes Pauen
Johannes Pauen has been a co-owner and managing director of kleiner und bold since 2008. He and his team are specialized on brand building for hidden champions. An economics graduate, he began his career as a cultural manager in Berlin in 1992. Since 1999, he has held senior managerial positions as a communications and branding consultant at various agencies. Since then, he worked with clients from the automobile, mechanical engineering, telecommunications, chemical industry, consumer goods and cultural sectors. Johannes works mainly on the design of strategy, services and implementation processes, as well as the design of spatial branding. He makes regular appearances to specialised audiences as an author and speaker on the topic of brand building and implementation and is a member of Deutscher Designer Club (DDC).

Dr. Cornelius Ringe

Cornelius studied business administration at the University of Augsburg with major in advertising psychology and gained his PhD with his dissertation about "Brand Artist Partnerships" at the department of Musicology and Media Science at Humboldt-Universität zu Berlin. After some experience in music business at Universal Music, he first worked as brand consultant at the audio consulting group. Afterwards he was consultant at Jung von Matt/brand identity. In 2009, Cornelius founded with his fellows Kai Bronner and Rainer Hirt the Audio Branding Academy in Hamburg. As guest lecturer Cornelius introduced audio branding as subject at the Pop Academy Baden-Wuerttemberg. As author of publications concerning audio branding and brand artist partnership his general field of research is sound identity, the meaning of music and sound in brand communications.

Julia Schwieger

Following an initial position as general business administrator, Julia Schwieger studied Event Marketing and worked three years as a project manager in this field. For the next six years Julia gained her main professional experience at the worldwide branding agency The Brand Union. Initially as a consultant in strategy, then moving into business development. As Julia Schwieger is especially interested in music she decided to combine her private passion with her professional background in branding. This led her to the audio consulting group where she works as consultant and marketing manager.

Professor Dr. Charles Spence

Professor Charles Spence is the head of the Crossmodal Research Laboratory at the Department of Experimental Psychology, Oxford University. He is interested in how people perceive the world around them. In particular, how our brains manage to process the information from each of our different senses to form the extraordinarily rich multisensory experiences that fill our daily lives. His research focuses on how a better understanding of the human mind will lead to the better design of auditory and multisensory products, brands, interfaces, and environments in the future. Charles has acted as a consultant for a number of multinational companies advising on various aspects of sensory design, including Unilever, Procter & Gamble, ICI, McDonalds, Starbucks, Quest, Firmenich, Britvic, Neurosense, Starbucks and The Fat Duck restaurant.

Diana Tobias

Diana Tobias is a student of Popular Music and Media at the University of Paderborn in Germany. Besides her musical activities like playing the piano and conducting choirs, she has experiences in recording music and organizing musical events. Due to her studies she became interested in media production while working for the university radio station "Campusradio L'Unico" as an editor, host and second chairman. Furthermore, she worked in different media productions, especially in photography and film. In this context she took an interest in aesthetics, mode of operation and effects of film and advertising music.

Julian Treasure

Julian is author of the book Sound Business, and he has been widely featured in the world's media. His TED talks on sound have been viewed an estimated five million times: he is one of very few speakers in the world with four talks on TED.com. Julian is chairman of The Sound Agency, a UK-based consultancy that helps clients like BBC, BP, Coca-Cola, Harrods and Waldorf Astoria achieve better results by optimising the sound they make – for example by auditing, defining and creating BrandSound™, or by designing and installing effective and appropriate soundscapes in spaces such as shops, offices and corporate receptions.

Carlos Velasco

Carlos Velasco is a DPhil student of Experimental Psychology at the Crossmodal Research Laboratory, Department of Experimental Psychology, University of Oxford. He has participated in both academic and industrial congresses such as SPSP, SXSW and ESOMAR, and his research has been published in journals such as Food Quality and Preference. He is the former CEO and one of the co-founders of NEUROSKETCH, a Colombian company that conducts applied research in the field of consumer psychology and neuroscience for organizations. He has worked with companies such as Microsoft, SABMiller, Takasago, Givaudan, Terpel and many other national and multinational companies in South America in a variety of topics such as multisensory design, packaging, branding, advertising and marketing.

Lydia Watson

A recent member of The Sound Agency team, Lydia is now a firm devotee of the power of audio branding and the benefits of using applied sound for business. With a background in Client Services, Lydia brings her years of experience managing complex and demanding relationships with large corporate organisations, multi-nationals and high net-worth individuals to the world of audio consultancy, helping her clients to achieve better results by optimising the sound they make in every aspect of their business and achieving congruency across their brand as a whole. Lydia holds a BA in Middle Eastern Studies with Classical Greek from Exeter University and is passionate about opera and learning new languages. Working so closely with Harrods, one of the world's most famous retail stores, whilst The Sound Agency continues to create award-winning sounds, is truly a dream come true.

Alexander Wodrich

After receiving his university degree in business and marketing communications, Alexander launched his career at the Frankfurt-based advertising agency "Wunderman" (Young & Rubicam) in 1998, and later joined Germany's largest agency for branding and corporate identity, MetaDesign in Berlin, to work for clients such as DHL, Lufthansa and Volkswagen. In 2007 he became member of the management board at Germany's leading agency for branding and corporate identity, MetaDesign in Berlin. He founded his own audio branding consultancy in 2010. Alexander Wodrich is a regular speaker at congresses and a lecturer at different universities. His work has been honored with various awards. Just now he was nominated for the 2012 German Design Award for the audio branding of the French insurance provider AG2R La Mondiale.

In the following **company directory**, competent providers of audio branding services are listed. If you are looking for the right experts according to your project needs or have any further questions, please don't hesitate to contact the Audio Branding Academy for more information, help or advice: info@audio-branding-academy.org. Among others the Audio Branding Academy provides administration services like:

- Selection and recommendation of agencies and experts
- Support and supervision of pitches
- Composing of pitch briefs
- Setting up evaluation criteria and scoring systems
- Analysis of pitch presentations

Company Directory

amp GmbH – audible brand and corporate communication

Sandstr. 33   +49 89 2323899 0
80335, Munich   mail@ampcontact.com
Germany   www.ampcontact.com

Schönenbergstrasse 22   +41 78 762 2145
8820 Wädenswil-Zürich   mail@ampcontact.ch
Switzerland   www.ampcontact.ch

Type of company:	Audible brand and corporate communication agency
Founded:	2008
Employees:	4
Services:	Full-service agency for corporate music and sound: consulting, strategy, research, production, implementation and evaluation

About the company

We combine business intelligence and emotions with music. We translate strategically these emotions for brand communication, marketing and advertising. We achieve lasting recognition for brands and thus strengthen their identity. We take a rational approach. But we get emotional results. Music knows no limits. Nor does our thinking. We make ideas real. Especially ideas no one has come up with yet. We believe in our work. That's why our clients believe in us.

Clients

BMW, MINI, The Linde Group, BSH Bosch und Siemens Hausgeräte, Mercedes Benz, Bavaria Film, China Club Berlin, Lufthansa, Heinrich Bauer Media, Heye & Partner / BBDO, McDonald's Deutschland, The Walt Disney Company (Germany), ZDF, Goethe-Institut, Munich Fabric Start.

Audio Clusters

117, avenue Victor Hugo
92100 Boulogne Billancourt
France

Tel. +33 (0)1 70 96 00 16
Fax +33 (0)1 70 96 00 99
info@audioclusters.com
www.audioclusters.com

Type of company:

Audio branding agency, Music Productions, Music Publishing

Founded:

2012

Services:

Audio Branding (Consulting, Creation, Continuity), Holistic Audio Identity TM

About the company

Our goal is to provide the best Audio Branding Service, in the areas of Consulting, Creation and Continuity of the process. We are committed to delivering a high level of Consulting, by using a holistic approach method, scientifically structured, and continuously improved through research funding and the constant monitoring of Audio Branding innovations. We offer a new approach to Creation, thanks to our creators' different cultural backgrounds. Our team's commitment is to offer the certainty of Continuity, of a sealed and specific sound. An Audio Identity that expresses it self through time.

Clients

RTS, M6, TF1, NISSAN, MLD, Emergeances, SEMELI Resort, GlobalpreSense, American College, Eurecom.

audity

audity GbR

Blarerstraße 56	Tel +49 7531 36 38 524
78462 Konstanz	Fax +49 7531 20 05 22
Germany	info@audity.info
	www.audity.info

Type of company:	Agency for audio branding, audio interaction and audio experience
Founded:	2006
Employees:	3
Services:	Audible communication for brands, companies and products

About the company

audity is an agency for auditory communications based in Konstanz. The agency makes brands and companies resound via audio logos or jingles and develops acoustic signs that facilitate communication between man and machine. Through publications about audio branding, the online platform www.audio-branding.de or the unique international expert network for acoustic brand communication ICAB, audity gives strong impetus to the industry. Managing partner Rainer Hirt is jury member of the renowned red-dot-awards in the category "sounddesign & audio branding" and founder member of the Audio Branding Academy. audity is a "Ausgewählter Ort 2010" of the initiative "Deutschland – Land der Ideen."

Clients

Bosch-Siemens-Hausgeräte, Danone, Symrise, Volkswagen AG.

B Sound Thinking

Alameda Coelho Neto, 99	Tel +55 51 3335 3504
Porto Alegre 91340-340	paulo@somosb.st
Brazil	www.somosb.st

Type of company:	Audio Branding, Audio Advertising and Audio Interactive Company
Founded:	2003
Employees:	14
Services:	We are experts in brand strategic sound alignment consultancy, where we develop and manage the brand's sonic identity. We also produce and record sound and music for advertising, digital environments, performance and transmedia composing.

About the company

Not mere executors. Instead, a creative force. Not simply adding sound to an advert. Instead, contributing to its storytelling. Replacing the plain production, deeper sound thinking, in any media. Rather than just delivering the soundtrack of a campaign, thinking the development of a sound concept. Instead of a process, a direction: Sound Thinking, mixing audio advertising, audio branding and audio interactive. Constantly thinking about new sound textures, new formats and even new sound technologies. We are curious and restless. We are B.

Clients

Coca-Cola, Johnson & Johnson, Reebok, Wal-Mart, Petrobras, GM, Kraft Foods, Lacta, Claro, Tim, FIAT, Greendene, Boticário, Olympikus. Airela (audio branding project developed in partnership with Domíniu and Zooma).

comevis GmbH & Co. KG

Schanzenstraße 23	Tel +49 (0) 221 – 95 64 90 510
51063 Cologne	Fax +49 (0) 0800 – 60 70 80 399
Germany	infoservice@comevis.com
	www.comevis.com
Type of company:	Audio branding, service design, customer experience
Founded:	2002
Employees:	18
Services:	Consultancy, production, licensing

About the company

comevis positions companies, brands and products in an acoustic manner. Increasingly, the correct tones decide on the success of the communication & dialog design, because smart sound concepts offer new possibilities of multi-sensory addressing. As a premium provider, we develop exceptional sound concepts in the fields of audio branding, audio marketing and audio interface design. We design service interfaces and dialog concepts so that these are usable and desirable from a customer's point of view. comevis delivers resonant customer experiences. We offer a comprehensive portfolio for all areas in which voice and sound lead to audio-supported emotionalization. The sound makes the difference and our passion is creating specific attitudes and atmospheres through smart sound concepts.

Clients

AIDA Cruises, Berge & Meer, BOSCH, Bundesministerium für Familie, BASE, Condor, Camlog, Continental, DB Schenker, Deutsche BKK, Deutsche Post, E-Plus Gruppe, GRUNDIG, HAMBURG ENERGIE, HypoVereinsbank, Meissen®, Management Circle, NetCologne, Öger Tours, Océ, QIAGEN, Sparkasse, Telekom Deutschland, Unity Media, VELUX, WGV Versicherung, Yves Rocher.

eliasarts

Elias Arts LLC

10 East 33rd St.	Tel 917-267-2912
Fourth Floor	Fax 212-226-8100
New York, NY 10016	saminoff@eliasarts.com
USA	www.eliasarts.com

Type of company:	Audio Identity, Music & Sound Design and Production
Founded:	1980
Employees:	25-50
Services:	Audio Identity, Strategy, Research, Design and Implementation; Brand-based original composition

About the company

Elias Arts is the pre-eminent Audio Identity, Branding and Strategy firm. Intellectual capital includes: proprietary processes and proven solutions that generate demonstrable ROI for brands across all touchpoints, 30 years expertise in music and sound design, validated best practices and points of view. Landmark research study on Audio Branding fielded in collaboration with sensory branding guru Martin Lindstrom in 2010; covered extensively in press. Solutions developed in collaboration with the legendary, highly awarded Elias Arts music production division (which works with 700 of Fortune 1,000 Co's).

Clients

Identity clients include: Audi, American Express, Cisco, Citi, Coca-Cola, Columbia Pictures, Cartoon Network, Comcast XFINITY, Dell, ESPN, Harrah's, Hillcrest Labs, IBM, Living Social, MTV, Nike, 1996 Summer Olympics, Orange Wireless, Palm, Pinnacle Entertainment, Sun Microsystems, The Travelers Companies, Trident, Verizon, Visa, Yahoo!

Flyabit

Fray Junípero Serra 27, L3-2   Tel +34 91 484 03 90
28039 Madrid   info@flyabit.es
Spain   www.flyabit.es

Type of company: Sound Branding Studio
Founded: 2012
Employees: 5-10
Services: Audio Branding, Music Supervision,
                               Music Composition, Sound Design,
                               Sound & Music for Advertising, TV &
                               Film, Sound Studio, Sonic Identity.

About the company

We build brands through the audio environment. We create meaningful experiences based on soundscapes and are experts in the use of sound and music as an efficient marketing tool. We balance a large experience in the advertising and branding industries with a solid career in the music and audio ones. Our team experience include advertising, audio branding, music publishing, music supervision, audio design, music composition & production, recording studio, sound tracking, audio for Film & Tv, retail or digital environments' design.

Clients

Telefónica, Línea Directa, Saffron (A1, M-Tel), Grey (Loterías del Estado), Havas Group (Nivea, El Corte Inglés, Bezoya, Hyundai).

Gomus

Estrada da Gávea 81

22451-263 Rio de Janeiro – RJ

Brazil

Tel: +55 21 3627-9261

gomus@gomus.com.br

www.gomus.com.br

Type of company: Audio Branding Agency

Founded: 2010

Employees: 13

Services: Audio Branding Consultancy, Retail Music Programming, Original Production, Special Projects

About the company

We are an Audio Branding agency based in Brazil, specialized in creating music experiences and developing brand identity through music. Alongside our clients, we study brand value, objectives, target audience and communication channels, valuing emotions and sensory aspects as important marketing tools. We use music as the focus and starting point for our work, in order to transform the way in which brands and people relate. Our work ranges from audio branding consultancy and mapping, retail music programming through our exclusive software, to original music production at our studios for film, television, advertising campaigns and fashion shows, and special audio experience projects.

Clients

Some of our clients: Coca-Cola, TV Globo, Globosat, Fiat, Eletrobrás, Osklen, Diesel (Brazil), The North Face (Brazil), Bodytech, Antonio Bernardo, New Order, Auslander, Isabela Capeto, Hoteis Marina, Eclectic, TEDx, Rádio GNT, Adriana Degreas, FYI Store, Lenny, Pop Up Store, Zazá Bistrô, Toulon, Quadrucci, Zuka.

GROVES Sound Communications

Isekai 20	Tel +49 40 47 10 35 0
20249 Hamburg	Fax +49 40 46 40 78
Germany	information@groves.de
	www.groves.de

Type of company:	Music and sound consultancy, production
Founded:	1984
Employees:	10
Services:	Consulting, production, composition, studios, licensing

About the company

With over 25 years of experience in communicating with music and sound, GROVES is acknowledged as a market leader in this field. Due to the increasing necessity for a systematic development process for Sound Identities, a separate division, GROVES Sound Branding, was formed in 1997. Our motto: "Your Sound. Everywhere. Always."

Clients

GROVES Sound Communications is proud to have worked for national and international brands and companies like e.g. LBS, EnBW, DATEV, Gerolsteiner, OLYMPUS, TUI, Dea, Wrigleys, Mentos, Bacardi, Winterthur, Audi, Nivea, Visa as well as several radio and TV stations.

iV LLC / iV2 GmbH

622 Hamilton Avenue
Nashville, TN 37203
USA

Tel +1.615.320.1444
skeller@ivgroup.cc
http://blog.ivgroup.cc

Schmickstr. 18
D-60314 Frankfurt
Germany

Tel +49.69.99999.300.82
ureese@ivgroup.cc

Type of company: Audio Branding
Founded: 2005
Employees: 5
Services: Audio branding: strategy, execution and
                     evaluation

About the company

iV is a creative community of audio and marketing professionals, focused on providing strategic audio branding for a wide range of global agencies and brands. With an emphasis on strategy, execution, evaluation and asset management, we offer our clients a suite of services that include consultation, education, measurement, music supervision, original music production, re-recording, audio logo development, music licensing, rights negotiation, sound design, audio UX/UI design, branded content, audio post production and more.

Clients

Opel, Ritter Sport, Audi, McDonalds, TUI, Nestea, Trojan, Dodge, Burger King, Toyota, Coca Cola, Ford, AT&T, Deutsche Bahn, Clausthaler, Melitta, Union Investment, Fidelity, Mercedes, PODS, SEAT, Telekom, Commerzbank.

RED ROCK PRODUCTION

Red Rock Production

Klenzestrasse 1 A	Tel +49 8158 99 55 -0
82327 Tutzing	Fax +49 8158 99 55 -99
Lake Starnberg	office@redrock.de
Germany	www.redrock.de

Type of company:	Music Production Company
Founded:	1986
Employees:	12
Services:	Composing, Production, Branded Entertainment & Sound Branding, Corporate Live-Shows and Events

About the company

With great experience and innovative concepts Red Rock Production is creating and producing music, live-shows & events, sound branding, audio-logos and film-scores for international companies and provides their clients with outstanding quality in the whole field of branded entertainment. Leslie Mandoki, founder and owner of Red Rock Production, is working with all major record-labels, the biggest film-companies and international superstars like Lionel Richie, Phil Collins, David Garrett and many more since years. Numerous projects, live concerts and huge corporate live-events, studio albums and his collaboration with Disney and DreamWorks as musical director for movies like "Mulan", "Tarzan" and "Atlantis" make him an experienced and visionary expert to match the needs of companies from all over the world in every detail.

Clients

Volkswagen Group, VW, Audi, Seat, Skoda, Bentley, Bugatti, Lamborghini, Porsche, Sixt, VDA, CDU, FC-Bayern München, Allianz, Segmueller, Disney, Bavaria Film.

Company Directory

soundlounge

48 Broadley Terrace	Tel +44 20 77 24 24 20
London NW1 6LG	Fax +44 20 77 06 10 25
England	Ruth@soundlounge.co.uk
	www.soundlounge.co.uk

Type of company:	Music Agency
Founded:	1980
Employees:	8
Services:	Music Supervision, Brand Sound, Procurement, Music Licensing, Music Composition & Production, Consumer Research

About the company

For over three decades, soundlounge has been working with brands to generate powerful and creative music solutions. We know that brand sound is more than a sonic logo, it is a comprehensive approach to all aspects of sound; sound audits, consumer response and market analysis. We enable brands to discover and understand their own unique sound DNA – characteristics that are as fundamental as font, colour, logo and packaging. This ensures that what the consumer already understands about the brand is always reflected in what they hear.

Clients

Leo Burnett Group, JWT London, AMV BBDO, Euro RSCG, M&C Saatchi, Austin Reed, New Look, Bacardi, Pandora Jewellery.

soundscape

Polonceaukade 10	Tel +31 6295 130 72
1014 DA Amsterdam	tina@soundscape.nl
The Netherlands	www.soundscape.nl

Type of company:	Music House
Founded:	1989
Employees:	The Netherlands (6), Germany (4), England (3)
Services:	Music Consultancy, Audio Branding, Composition, Production, Research and Licensing

About the company

Founded in 1989 as one of the first Music Houses in advertising and TV Soundscape has developed and produced music for hundreds of brands and campaigns all over the world. Our idea has always been that composing for a brand is impossible without consideration of the brand values. Throughout these years we developed ourselves in experts in translating these brand values into sonic guidelines and therefore helping brands to gain more from a marketing instrument they are already using. With a big international pool of A-list composers and musicians and a team of music and marketing experts we always try to find the fine balance between creativity and marketing science. In our humble opinion that's what audio branding is all about.

Clients

Proctor & Gamble, Volkswagen, Mercedes, O2, Reebok, Braun, Nike, T-Mobile, Unilever, BMW, Samsung, Nestle, Volvo, W!games, Endemol, BBDO and VCCP.

the art and science of sound

The Sound Agency

3000 Hillswood Drive Chertsey	Tel +44 845 500 2511
Surrey KT16 0RS	info@thesoundagency.com
UK	www.thesoundagency.com

Type of company:	Sound branding agency
Founded:	2003
Employees:	6+ (varies according to project)
Services:	BrandSound™ **consultancy** (sound audits, workshops, guidelines); **creative** (all sonic assets, especially generative soundscapes); **delivery** (Ambifier™ generative system)

About the company

The Sound Agency is the Audio Branding Award-winning innovator of BrandSound™, pioneer of generative retail soundscapes, and a full-service sound branding agency. Our founder Julian Treasure is a leading authority on sound and branding. He wrote the book *Sound Business*, speaks internationally, and is often featured in global media (e.g. *The Economist, TIME Magazine, Wall Street Journal*). His four TED.com talks on sound have been viewed by more than five million people.

Clients

Some of our clients: Harrods, BBC, Capital Shopping Centres, Coca-Cola, Hammerson, Helm Bank, Honda, mfi, Nokia, BP, Waldorf Astoria, Biamp Systems.

WESOUND

Agency for Auditory Brand Development

WESOUND GmbH

Altonaer Straße 1	Tel +49 30 221 943 590
10557 Berlin	Fax +49 30 221 943 599
Germany	berlin@wesound.de
	www.wesound.de

Type of company:	Agency for Auditory Brand Development
Founded:	2011
Employees:	7
Services:	Consultancy, development and design of auditory brand appearances

About the company

WESOUND was founded in 2011 by Carl-Frank Westermann and Andreas Arntzen as a specialized agency for auditory brand develop-ment, with offices in Berlin and Hamburg. WESOUND offers consultancy, development and design of auditory brand appearances in different fields: Sound Branding for TV and Radio purposes, product and interaction sounds or scenographic sound design for virtual and physical spaces. WESOUND consists of a core team of sound specialists with backgrounds in a variety of disciplines. The WESOUND team's passion for sound, its creativity, its professional network, and its track record of success make the new agency uniquely able to respond individually and flexibly to market and project requirements.

Clients

Brands like ARAG , BAYER, JUNGHEINRICH, SEAT, SIEMENS or YAPITAL.

WODRICH
I I I I I I I I I AUDIO
I I I I BRANDING

Wodrich Audio Branding

Milastr. 2   Tel +49 – 30 – 787 737 - 27
10437 Berlin   Fax +49 – 30 – 787 737 - 37
Germany   aw@wodrich-audio-branding.de
                               www.wodrich-audio-branding.de

Type of company: Audio branding agency
Founded: 2010
Employees: 7
Services: Strategic brand consulting, audio-
                              production, design, motion graphics

About the company

Wodrich Audio Branding's strategic approach transforms a brand's personality into sound and implements its audio-identity at all touch-points. The agency offers the full service package with research, audit, strategy, audio-production, graphic-design, motion-graphics, implementation and testing. In the last three years Wodrich Audio Branding has been honoured with a red-dot-design-award, the audio branding award in silver, a German Design Award nomination as well as a CREA award. Before founding Wodrich Audio Branding, Alexander Wodrich was the "Head of Sound Branding" and a member of the management board at Germany's leading design agency MetaDesign in Berlin.

Clients

Siemens Enterprise Communications, Deutsche Bahn, FIFA, AG2R La Mondiale, DKSH, Wiener Linien, AVM, IHK, CLAAS, Bayer Health Care.

Zanna Sound

R. Eng. Marques Porto, 104-202	Rio: +55.21.2246.0400
Lagoa – Rio de Janeiro	SP: +55.119.7989.0400
Brazil	talktozanna@zanna.net
	www.zanna.net

Type of company:	Sound agency
Founded:	2006
Employees:	6
Services:	Sound Branding

About the company
Founded in Rio de Janeiro in 2006, Zanna Sound is Latin America's first Sound Branding agency and the first to speak on this topic at the Cannes Lions Festival – France 2012. We can now say that we created the Sound Branding category in Latin America through all the content we've developed over the years with lectures, articles, TV programs and internet videos, and with our tireless participation in advertising festivals and active presence on the market through the presentation of significant cases. We have disseminated this new indispensable tool and helped our clients understand the need to have their own sound and make brands recognizable by sound alone. Today, everyone respects and covets the Sound Branding category.

Clients
Banco do Brasil, Embratur, Sabesp, MetroRio, GRU Airport, Vivo, Ponto Frio, Marie Claire, Veet, TIM Mobile, Grupo Boticario e L'Oreal.